Project Management Fundamentals

(Second Edition)

Project Management Fundamentals: (Second Edition)

Part Number: 084018
Course Edition: 1.1

NOTICES

DISCLAIMER: While Element K Corporation takes care to ensure the accuracy and quality of these materials, we cannot guarantee their accuracy, and all materials are provided without any warranty whatsoever, including, but not limited to, the implied warranties of merchantability or fitness for a particular purpose. The name used in the data files for this course is that of a fictitious company. Any resemblance to current or future companies is purely coincidental. We do not believe we have used anyone's name in creating this course, but if we have, please notify us and we will change the name in the next revision of the course. Element K is an independent provider of integrated training solutions for individuals, businesses, educational institutions, and government agencies. Use of screenshots, photographs of another entity's products, or another entity's product name or service in this book is for editorial purposes only. No such use should be construed to imply sponsorship or endorsement of the book by, nor any affiliation of such entity with Element K. This courseware may contain links to sites on the Internet that are owned and operated by third parties (the "External Sites"). Element K is not responsible for the availability of, or the content located on or through, any External Site. Please contact Element K if you have any concerns regarding such links or External Sites.

TRADEMARK NOTICES Element K and the Element K logo are trademarks of Element K Corporation and its affiliates.

Copyright © 2009 Element K Corporation. All rights reserved. Screenshots used for illustrative purposes are the property of the software proprietor. This publication, or any part thereof, may not be reproduced or transmitted in any form or by any means, electronic or mechanical, including photocopying, recording, storage in an information retrieval system, or otherwise, without express written permission of Element K, 500 Canal View Boulevard, Rochester, NY 14623, (585) 240-7500, (800) 478-7788. Element K Courseware's World Wide Web site is located at www.elementkcourseware.com.

This book conveys no rights in the software or other products about which it was written; all use or licensing of such software or other products is the responsibility of the user according to terms and conditions of the owner. Do not make illegal copies of books or software. If you believe that this book, related materials, or any other Element K materials are being reproduced or transmitted without permission, please call (800) 478-7788.

Your comments are important to us. Please contact us at Element K Press LLC, 1-800-478-7788, 500 Canal View Boulevard, Rochester, NY 14623, Attention: Product Planning, or through our Web site at http://support.elementkcourseware.com.

Project Management Fundamentals: (Second Edition)

Lesson 1: Getting Started with Project Management
    A. Describe a Project 2
    B. Describe the Project Management Life Cycle 6
    C. Identify the Role of a Project Manager 11

Lesson 2: Initiating a Project
    A. Determine the Scope of a Project 20
    B. Identify the Skills for a Project Team 27
    C. Identify the Risks to a Project 33

Lesson 3: Planning for Time and Cost
    A. Create a Work Breakdown Structure 40
    B. Sequence the Activities..................................... 44
    C. Create a Project Schedule................................... 51
    D. Determine Project Costs.................................... 62

Lesson 4: Planning for Project Risks, Communication, and Change Control
    A. Analyze the Risks to a Project............................... 68
    B. Create a Communication Plan 72
    C. Plan for Change Control 75

Lesson 5: Managing a Project
    A. Begin Project Work 80

B. Execute the Project Plan 83
C. Track Project Progress 86
D. Report Performance 93
E. Implement Change Control 97

Lesson 6: Executing the Project Closeout Phase

A. Close a Project 102
B. Create a Final Report 105

Lesson Labs 111

Solutions 121

Glossary 149

Index 151

About This Course

Successfully managing a project requires effective planning and adherence to the industry's best practices in every step of the process. By understanding the fundamentals of project management, you will be better prepared to initiate a project in your organization and position it for success. In this course, you will identify effective project management practices and their related processes.

At this point in your professional development, you are ready to take on the responsibility for managing projects. You can manage a project by developing a solid understanding of the fundamentals of project management and its underlying structure and elements, including project phases, project life cycles, stakeholders, and areas of expertise. These, coupled with the ability to identify the project management processes that are recognized industry-wide as good practice, will help you to apply effective project management techniques to improve the efficiency of your projects and ensure their success.

Course Description

Target Student

This course is designed for individuals whose primary job is not project management, but who manage projects on an informal basis. Also, anyone who is considering a career path in project management and desiring a complete overview of the field and its generally accepted practices can take up this course.

Course Prerequisites

To ensure your success, it is recommended that you first take the following Element K courses: *Word 2000, Word 2002, Word 2003*, or *Microsoft® Office Word® 2007: Level 1;* or have equivalent knowledge. Some on-the-job experience in participating in managed projects would be preferable.

How to Use This Book

As a Learning Guide

Each lesson covers one broad topic or a set of related topics. Lessons are arranged in the order of increasing proficiency with *project management fundamentals*; skills you acquire in one lesson are used and developed in subsequent lessons. For this reason, you should work through the lessons in sequence.

We organized each lesson into result-oriented topics. Topics include all the relevant and supporting information you need to master *project management fundamentals*, and activities allow you to apply this information to practical hands-on examples.

You get to try out each new skill on a specially prepared sample file. This saves you typing time and allows you to concentrate on the skill at hand. Through the use of sample files, hands-on activities, illustrations that give you feedback at crucial steps, and supporting background information, this book provides you with the foundation and structure to learn *project management fundamentals* quickly and easily.

As a Review Tool

Any method of instruction is only as effective as the time and effort you are willing to invest in it. In addition, some of the information that you learn in class may not be important to you immediately, but it may become important later on. For this reason, we encourage you to spend some time reviewing the topics and activities after the course. For additional challenge when reviewing activities, try the "What You Do" column before looking at the "How You Do It" column.

As a Reference

The organization and layout of the book make it easy to use as a learning tool and as an after-class reference. You can use this book as a first source for definitions of terms, background information on given topics, and summaries of procedures.

Course Icons

Icon	Description
	A **Caution Note** makes students aware of potential negative consequences of an action, setting, or decision that are not easily known.
	Display Slide provides a prompt to the instructor to display a specific slide. Display Slides are included in the Instructor Guide only.
	An **Instructor Note** is a comment to the instructor regarding delivery, classroom strategy, classroom tools, exceptions, and other special considerations. Instructor Notes are included in the Instructor Guide only.
	Notes Page indicates a page that has been left intentionally blank for students to write on.
	A **Student Note** provides additional information, guidance, or hints about a topic or task.
	A **Version Note** indicates information necessary for a specific version of software.

Course Objectives

In this course, you will examine the elements of sound project management and apply the generally recognized practices to successfully manage projects.

You will:

- identify the key processes and requirements of project management.
- initiate a project.
- plan for time and cost.
- plan for project risks, communication, and change control.
- manage a project.
- execute the project closeout phase.

Course Requirements

Hardware
- Intel® Pentium® IV 300 MHz processor
- 64 MB RAM with 1.0 GB free hard disk space
- CD-ROM drive
- Super VGA recommended (set at least to 800 x 600 screen resolution) with 256 colors
- An Internet connection

Software
The instructor's computer should have the following software:
- Microsoft® PowerPoint® 2000 or later

Class Setup

Classroom setup requires one computer for the instructor. Students do not require computers.

List of Additional Files

Printed with each activity is a list of files students open to complete that activity. Many activities also require additional files that students do not open, but are needed to support the file(s) students are working with. These supporting files are included with the student data files on the course CD-ROM or data disk. Do not delete these files.

If your book did not come with a CD, please go to **http:// www.elementk.com/ courseware-file-downloads** to download the data files.

1 Getting Started with Project Management

Lesson Time: 1 hour(s), 5 minutes

Lesson Objectives:

In this lesson, you will identify the key processes and requirements of project management.

You will:

- Describe the characteristics of a project.
- Describe the project management life cycle.
- Identify the role of a project manager.

Introduction

You actively participated in a project. Now, you want to move from participating in projects to managing projects. In this lesson, you will be introduced to the basic terminology used in project management, examine the phases in a project's life cycle, and identify the roles and responsibilities of a project manager.

To be a successful project manager, you need to be able to use your management skills with a sound knowledge of the processes to achieve your goals. By identifying the key elements of effective project management practice, you can enhance your chances of success in managing a wide range of projects across application areas and industries.

TOPIC A
Describe a Project

Before you begin to play a role in managing a project, you need to know everything about the project in detail. In this topic, you will define a project and identify its characteristics.

Business organizations around the world are using project management as a competitive advantage to achieve corporate strategic objectives. Before beginning to apply the principles of project management on your job, you need to know what a project is and how it is different from other day-to-day activities.

Projects

Definition:

A *project* is a temporary endeavor that creates a unique product, service, or result. It has a clearly defined duration. It develops in steps and continues to grow in increments. The end of a project is reached when either its objectives are met, the need for the project no longer exists, or it is determined that the objectives cannot be met. Projects can vary widely in terms of budget, team size, duration, expected outcomes, and industries.

Example: Project Authorized to Develop a Word Processor

Consider a project authorized by a software firm to develop a new version of a word processor. The outcome of the project is the word processor application. The duration of the project depends on the complexity and size of the work involved and the organization's business objectives. The project will come to an end when the product is ready for distribution in the market.

Operational Tasks and Projects

Operational tasks are ongoing and repetitive tasks that produce the same outcome every time they are performed, whereas projects are temporary endeavors with a unique outcome. While the purpose of operational tasks is to carry out day-to-day activities and sustain the business, the purpose of projects is to meet specific objectives. Projects conclude when their objectives are met, but operational tasks adopt new objectives and the work continues.

The Project Life Cycle

Projects are typically broken down into manageable, sequential phases of work activities to improve management control. Those *project phases,* taken together, are referred to as the *project life cycle.* Project life cycles may have four or five phases, which vary in the customized life cycle versions. The project life cycle is marked by the beginning and the end of the project. During the initial phase, the project's objectives and timing are determined. During the intermediate phases, detailed planning occurs along with the actual work activities. In the final phase, project-closing activities occur.

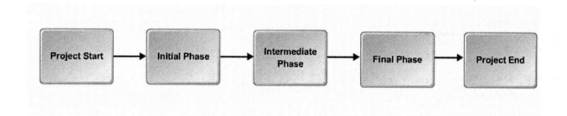

Need for a Project

Projects serve as a means for carrying out activities that cannot be performed like the other operational tasks. They form a part of an organization's strategic plan and enable the organization to achieve the plan. An organization takes up a project based on strategic considerations, such as, an organizational need, a market demand, a customer request, a technological advancement, or a legal requirement.

Project Stakeholders

Definition:

A *project stakeholder* is a person who has a business interest in the outcome of a project. Project stakeholders exert influence on the objectives of a project. Their expectations and needs have to be identified and met for a project to deliver a successful outcome. They have different responsibilities and command varying levels of authority over a project.

Example: Project Stakeholders for a Construction Project

David Anderson, the project manager is supervising the expansion of a large municipal public library. Stakeholders in this project include government agencies, taxpayers, the voters who has voted to authorize the city to issue bonds for the project, and private donors who have contributed towards costs.

Types of Project Stakeholders

A project can have different types of stakeholders.

Project Stakeholder	Responsibility
Sponsor	An individual or group that provides financial resources for a project.
Customer	An individual or organization that will use the project's output and pays for it.
Project manager	An individual who is responsible for managing a project.
Project team	A group that performs the work on a project.
Project management team	The members of a project team who perform the project management activities.

ACTIVITY 1-1
Understanding a Project

Scenario:
You are coordinating a group of tax return processors. Everyday your team interviews clients, uses the data to fill out tax returns, and computes the amount of tax owed. You are asked to take on the additional responsibility of coordinating the team as the manager, Rita, is going on a vacation. The team is developing a training manual to help new tax return processors learn their jobs faster. Her team is made up of tax return specialists, writers, and graphic designers who are assigned to the team part-time. The work must be completed by January 1 in time for Human Resources to train the new tax return processors who will be hired next year.

1. Which is a characteristic of the project Rita's team is working on?
   a) Performs the day-to-day activities of a business.
   b) Produces the same output every time.
   c) Has a definite beginning and a definite end.
   d) Is ongoing and repetitive.

2. Match each stakeholder with the appropriate responsibility.

   ___ Project manager   a. An individual or group that provides financial resources for a project.

   ___ Customer   b. An individual or organization that will use the project's output.

   ___ Sponsor   c. An individual responsible for managing a project.

   ___ Project team   d. The members of the project team who perform project management activities.

   ___ Project management team   e. A group that performs the work in a project.

3. True or False? Your team of tax return processors is assigned an operational task.
   ___ True
   ___ False

4. True or False? Rita's team performs a set of repetitive tasks and there is no outcome. Therefore, they are assigned an ongoing work activity.
   ___ True
   ___ False

5. **True or False? Managing Rita's project may be more difficult than managing your group of tax return processors because this project work has never been undertaken before, the team is multidisciplined with conflicting priorities, and the team also reports to other managers.**

　__ True

　__ False

TOPIC B
Describe the Project Management Life Cycle

You defined a project and identified its characteristics. Before assuming project management responsibilities, you need to identify how project management functions within an organization and how it serves to achieve the objectives of the business. In this topic, you will describe the project management life cycle.

To perform project management duties successfully, you need to get a clear idea of what project management is, identify how an organization aligns the ongoing projects with its strategic goals, and analyze how a project is managed. For this, you need to define project, program, and portfolio management, and describe the project management life cycle.

Project Management

Definition:

Project management is the management of project activities to meet the project's objectives. It is accomplished through the application and integration of knowledge, skills, tools, and techniques to project activities. It does not only involve scheduling and getting the work done, but also includes identifying requirements; establishing objectives; balancing quality, scope, time and cost; and addressing the concerns and expectations of the stakeholders. Project management may differ from project to project considering the activities that need to be performed and the tools and techniques to be used.

Example: Project Management Involved in Building a New Refinery

Project management is required to manage the activities involved in building a new refinery authorized by an oil company. The project manager must grapple with communicating cross-functionally, manage the efforts of people who are external or internal to the company, and deliver the work on time, within the allotted budget, and within the specifications for quality.

Program

Definition:

A *program* is a group of related projects that may have a common objective. It offers greater control over the constituent projects and delivers benefits that the organization can utilize to meet its goals. A program is generally managed by a program manager, and the individual projects are managed by project managers who work for the program manager. In some organizations, a program is viewed as ongoing work without a clear end point.

Example: Program to Build a Residential Complex

OGC Builders has proposed a new program that involves building a large residential complex, which will include a number of smaller projects.

Program Management

Definition:
Program management is the management of a program in a centralized and coordinated manner to achieve the program's objectives and benefits. It involves managing work that is beyond the scope of the individual projects in a program. Program management includes managing multiple discrete projects and integrating them towards a common goal. It requires managers to manage the interdependencies between the projects by allocating resources, prioritizing efforts, and maintaining the projects' alignment with business objectives.

Example: The Apollo Program
The Apollo program's mission was to put a man on the moon within ten years. Apollo 1, 2, and 3 were short-term projects within the Apollo program.

Portfolio

Definition:
A *portfolio* is a collection of programs or projects that are grouped to achieve an organization's strategic business objectives. The projects in a portfolio may or may not be interdependent, but they are grouped to give the management a broader view of the organization's projects and their adherence to organizational objectives. For a project to be part of a portfolio, its attributes such as cost, requirement of resources, timelines, and benefits should be in line with the other projects in the portfolio and the strategic goals the portfolio is expected to meet. Portfolios are generally managed by a senior manager or senior management teams.

Example: Portfolio at OGC Energies
OGC Energies has started a portfolio that involves designing a breakthrough technology capitalizing on solar energy. This portfolio includes a number of smaller programs and projects; each of these smaller programs contains a series of projects.

Portfolio Management

Definition:
Portfolio management is the management of a portfolio to ensure that all projects in the portfolio contribute to achieving the organization's strategic goals. It allows managers a global, top-down view of the health and viability of all the projects in the portfolio. Portfolio management strives to maximize the value of a portfolio by carefully selecting projects to be included in the portfolio and excluding those that are not meeting the strategic objectives. Portfolio management may be different in each organization as it depends on the organizations' strategic objectives and business needs.

Example: Portfolio Management at a Construction Company
The senior management of a construction company uses portfolio management to manage their residential, commercial, and infrastructure-based projects. Their goal is to gain ground on residential projects while ensuring that the projects meet strategic objectives set by the organization.

Project Deliverable

Definition:
A *project deliverable* is an output from a project management activity that is measurable, unique, and verifiable. Project deliverables require the approval and sign-off of the project stakeholders. The deliverables of one phase of a project serve as inputs to the subsequent phase. The project manager and the stakeholders determine the project deliverables based on the size and requirements of a project.

Example: Project Deliverable of a Project at OGC Technologies
OGC Technologies, a software development company has proposed a project for updating a software with more features. The project deliverable of this project will be the final version of the updated software, the features of which will have to be approved by the customers, users, and other key stakeholders.

The Project Management Processes

Project management processes are all the activities that underlie the effective practice of project management. There are five processes in the project management life cycle. They are:

1. Initiation - Defines a project and formally authorizes its start.
2. Planning - Defines project objectives and scope, and plans the steps to be taken to meet those objectives.
3. Execution - Organizes the project team and carries out the tasks required to complete the project.
4. Monitoring and Controlling - Surveys project execution to identify problems, take corrective action, and ensure that the project is on track.
5. Closeout - Brings the project to a formal completion, irrespective of whether the objectives are met or not.

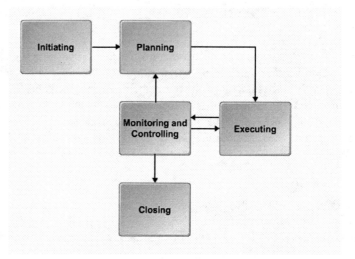

ACTIVITY 1-2
Understanding the Project Management Life Cycle

Scenario:
Having taken over the project on developing the training manual, you need to identify the project management activities and processes required to start the project. You need to establish an understanding of how the project is to be managed, analyze the outcome of each process, and figure out the activities the stakeholders need to be involved.

1. **Which definition best describes project management?**

   a) Management of a collection of programs to ensure that all projects in the collection contribute to achieving the organization's strategic goals.

   b) Management of project activities to meet project objectives through the application of knowledge, skills, tools, and techniques to those activities.

   c) Management of a collection of projects in a centralized and coordinated manner to achieve collective objectives and benefits.

   d) Management of day-to-day activities to sustain the business.

2. **Match each term with its definition.**

   ___ Project   a. Collection of related projects that may have a common objective.

   ___ Portfolio   b. A temporary endeavor that creates a unique product, service, or result.

   ___ Program   c. Collection of programs or projects that achieve an organization's strategic business objectives.

3. **Which is a project management process?**

   a) Verification

   b) Prototyping

   c) Planning

   d) Designing

4. **True or False? A project deliverable requires the approval and sign-off of project stakeholders.**

   ___ True

   ___ False

5. **Which project management process allows you to identify problems and take corrective action?**

    a) Monitoring and Controlling

    b) Execution

    c) Planning

    d) Initiation

6. **In which project management process will you define a project's objectives and plan for the course of action to be taken?**

    a) Initiation

    b) Execution

    c) Monitoring and Controlling

    d) Planning

TOPIC C
Identify the Role of a Project Manager

You know about projects and project management. Now, you may be wondering about how to use it to attain your objectives. In this topic, you will identify the role of a project manager.

A project manager will need to coordinate the work of the team members and interact with people from different functions. To be successful in project management, you need to possess many skills other than traditional management and communication skills. Having a clear idea of the required skills will help you gain an insight into your role as a project manager.

Skills of a Project Manager

A project manager needs to possess multiple skills in order to be successful. The skills of a project manager can be broadly classified into five categories.

Category	Description
Project management knowledge	<ul><li>Knowledge of project management tools and techniques.</li><li>Ability to apply the project management knowledge to ongoing projects.</li></ul>
Knowledge of the application area	<ul><li>Knowledge of the industry, functional departments, and technical elements.</li><li>Familiarity with accepted standards and regulations.</li></ul>
Understanding of the project environment	<ul><li>Understanding the impact of the project on the organization.</li><li>Familiarity with the laws that could affect a project.</li><li>Awareness of any physical impact a project may have on its physical environment.</li></ul>
General management knowledge and skills	<ul><li>Ability to plan, organize, staff, execute, and control operations.</li><li>Manage time.</li><li>Ability to estimate and budget.</li><li>Ability to manage risks.</li></ul>
Interpersonal skills	<ul><li>Ability to communicate with the senior management as well as the project team.</li><li>Ability to influence decisions.</li><li>Ability to lead a team.</li><li>Ability to motivate.</li><li>Ability to negotiate and manage conflicts.</li><li>Ability to solve problems.</li></ul>

Types of Organizational Structures

The organizational structure determines how the individuals in an organization are grouped, how project teams are structured, and the level of authority the project manager has over the team. There are four types of organizational structures.

Organizational Structure	Description
Functional	• A hierarchical organization in which each employee reports to a functional manager. • Employees are grouped based on their area of expertise. • A project team may comprise of members from different functions. • The authority of the project manager is lower compared to that of a functional manager.
Projectized	• An organization having many organizational units called departments with individuals in each department reporting directly to a project manager. • Employees are grouped based on the projects they are working on. • The project manager has complete control and authority over the project team.
Matrix	• An organization that follows a mix of the functional and projectized structures. • Individuals report directly to a functional manager but may also be controlled by a project manager. • A matrix structure can be characterized as strong, weak, or balanced based on the role of the project manager in the organization. • The authority of the project manager is greatest in a strong matrix structure and lowest in a weak matrix structure.
Composite	A combination of the Functional, Projectized, and Matrix structures. An organization may choose to follow a different structure at different levels of the hierarchy.

Project Management Office

A *Project Management Office* (PMO) is an administrative unit that supervises and coordinates the management of all projects in an organization. The focus of a PMO is to achieve the organization's business objectives by prioritizing and directing the execution of projects. The PMO strives to improve the project management performance of the organization by identifying best practices and maintaining standards across projects. It also serves as a central repository of project tools, project policies, procedures, templates, and other shared documentation. In addition, the PMO manages communication across projects, monitors project timelines, budget, and quality on an enterprise level, and provides a mentoring platform for project managers.

How to Identify the Role of a Project Manager

The overall success of a project depends largely on the role played by the project manager.

Guidelines

To be effective as a project manager, follow these guidelines:

- Apply project management knowledge to formalize project management.
    - Use project management tools and techniques to manage project activities.
    - Ensure that the project team follows standard processes.
    - Identify best practices and bring them into effect.
    - Ensure that the deliverables in each phase are acceptable.
- Apply knowledge of the application area to manage technical challenges.
    - Assess the technical competency of the project team, identify areas of concern, and train the team if required.
    - Ensure that the project meets accepted standards and regulations.
- Apply general management skills to successfully manage and control process responsibilities.
    - Manage the overall schedule of the project to ensure its successful completion on time.
    - Coordinate resources and motivate them to work towards the success of the project.
    - Identify and manage issues that arise in the project.
    - Monitor the project continuously to ensure that it meets the quality requirements.
    - Monitor project costs and ensure that the project is completed within budget.
- Apply knowledge of the project environment to assess the impact of the project on the organization.
    - Identify the impact of the project on the physical environment.
    - Identify the impact of the project on the organization's strategic plans.
    - Identify laws that could affect the project and take steps to minimize the impact.

- Apply interpersonal skills to successfully manage responsibilities of the resources.
    - Proactively communicate project information to the project team and the stakeholders.
    - Lead the team by clearly communicating your expectations.
    - Build the team as a disciplined unit that is focused on achieving the requirements of the project.
    - Resolve conflicts that may arise in the project.
- Take on additional responsibilities such as managing multiple projects or taking charge of all the documentation of a project.

Example: The Roles of a Project Manager in a Publishing Company

A project manager in a publishing company is assigned the task of bringing out a book on the basics of computers for children in the age group of 6 to 10 years. He needs to use project management tools to manage project activities and ensure that project deliverables meet the stakeholder's expectations. In order to ensure the successful completion of the project, the project manager needs to manage the overall project schedule, coordinate the resources, and monitor the project's quality continuously. He must also lead the team by clearly communicating necessary information and resolving conflicts while ensuring that the work is completed on time, within budget, and meets quality expectations.

DISCOVERY ACTIVITY 1-3
Identifying the Role of a Project Manager

Scenario:
Your company has taken up the task of publishing a cookbook, and you have been officially assigned as the manager for this project. The chef, Francesca Tosca, has been hired to create the recipes for Italian dishes. The project has already raised expectations in the market because Francesca is a famous TV personality. The project team will also include other cooks for assisting Francesca Tosca, writers, and graphic designers.

1. What skills do you require to ensure that the team is not bogged down by the market expectations and the superiority of Francesca Tosca?

    a) Culinary skills

    b) Good communication and negotiation skills

    c) Ability to motivate the team

    d) Complete project management knowledge

2. Francesca Tosca's popularity and her celebrity status may create a rift in the team if the rest of the team finds it difficult to handle her. In such a situation, what will be your role as project manager?

    a) Build the team as a disciplined unit that is focused on achieving the requirements of the project.

    b) Resolve conflicts that may arise in the project.

    c) Proactively communicate project information to the project team.

    d) Manage the overall schedule of the project to ensure its successful completion on time.

3. The cookbook team involves resources who perform different functions. Which organizational structure will give you the greatest control over the entire team?

    a) Composite

    b) Functional

    c) Matrix

    d) Projectized

4. **Francesca Tosca's TV schedules may frequently interfere with your project's schedules and affect the working hours of the other resources. What roles do you need to play to resolve this problem?**

   a) Manage the overall schedule of the project so that Francesca's TV schedules do not hamper the successful completion of the project.

   b) Proactively communicate project information to the project team and the stakeholders.

   c) Coordinate resources and motivate them to work toward the success of the project, in spite of the issues about the availability of the chef.

   d) Identify the impact of the project on the organization's strategic plans.

Lesson 1 Follow-up

In this lesson, you identified the key elements of project management. This enables you to enhance your chances of success in managing a wide range of projects across application areas and industries.

1. **Who are the stakeholders in the project you are currently working on? What are their expectations from the project?**

2. **What organizational structure does your company follow? What is the project manager's level of authority?**

2 Initiating a Project

Lesson Time: 1 hour(s)

Lesson Objectives:

In this lesson, you will initiate a project.

You will:
- Create a project scope statement.
- Identify the skills for a project team.
- Identify the risks to a project.

Introduction

You have a fair knowledge on the project life cycle and the skills required to be a project manager. Having understood the rudiments of project management, you are ready to get going with the initial stages of a project. In this lesson, you'll discover how to initiate a project, and perform the critical steps involved in laying the foundation for your project's success.

Starting a project is like starting a new job; the more you know about the company, your team members, and what is expected of you, the more likely you are to hit the ground running and make a good impression. Ensuring that your project starts out right will not only save you time and resources, but will also eliminate the need to backtrack once your project is officially underway.

TOPIC A
Determine the Scope of a Project

You are aware of the organizational objectives, business requirements, and the expected results of a project. Now, you are ready to initiate your project. Before you begin the planning process, you need to clearly identify the tasks involved in a project. In this topic, you will determine the scope of a project.

Clearly stating the work involved in a project helps the stakeholders to understand what needs to be accomplished to meet the project's objectives. Without that, they could end up spending valuable time and resources on work that isn't even supposed to be part of their project. With a clear scope statement, you will enable all participants and stakeholders to focus on the true goals of the project.

Scope Statement
Definition:
The *scope statement* is an itemized definition of the outcome of a project. It is derived from the information provided by the stakeholders of the project. It explains what is to be included and excluded from a project. The scope can change during the course of the project.

Example: A Sample Scope Statement

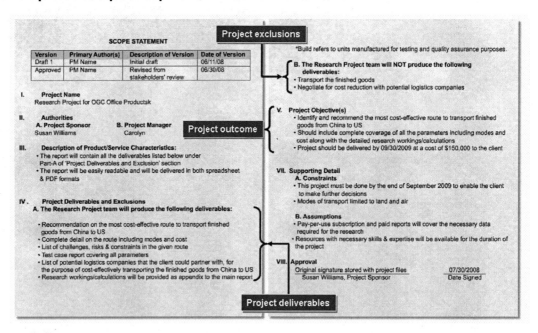

Scope Creep
Scope creep is the additional task items that are added to a project as the project progresses, and these items make it difficult to achieve project goals. Also, scope creep occurs when the project expands inappropriately without securing stakeholders approval or without addressing the effect that such expansion will have on the project's cost, time, and resources.

Constraining Factors

Constraining factors are the factors that limit the way a project can be approached. These limitations may concern time, cost, scope, quality, resources, and others. Of these, scope, cost, and time are considered as the three major constraining factors in every project. These factors are interrelated and exist in a state of equilibrium. As the project progresses, if one of these factors are altered, the other two factors should be balanced to accommodate the change without compromising the quality of the product or service.

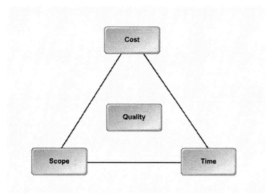

Figure 2-1: The constraints triangle.

Project Assumptions

Definition:

Project assumptions are statements that must be taken to be true in order for the project planning to begin. The project manager creates a list of assumptions for a project. The project benefits if the assumptions prove to be true and suffers if the assumptions are wrong. Therefore, as the project progresses, assumptions have to be reviewed and reworked to decide if they prove to be true.

Example: Common Project Assumptions

Some of the common project assumptions are:

- Project staff resources will be available as and when they are needed.
- Technical support will be available as and when they are needed.
- The scope of the project will remain unchanged.

Project Objectives

Definition:

Project objectives are the criteria used to measure whether a project is successful or not. Objectives must be:

- Realistic and attainable.
- Specific in terms of scope.
- Quantifiable in terms of time, cost, and quality.
- Consistent with organizational plans, policies, and procedures.

Projects may have one or several objectives, and subobjectives may be added to the project in order to further clarify the project goals.

Example: Objectives of an Add-in Component Project

The following objective was developed for a project on the development of an add-in component to a word processor application.

Develop an add-in component to the word processor application that provides advanced text-to-speech functions by October 31, 2009 at a cost of $200 for existing customers who already own a license to the application.

- The objective specifies the scope: Add-in component to a word processor application that provides advanced text-to-speech functions.
- Time: Development to be completed by October 31, 2009.
- Cost: $200.

The Scope Definition Process

The *scope definition process* allows project managers to document the project's parameters, its objectives, requirements, and deliverables in the project scope statement. There are several stages in this process.

Stage	Description
Step 1: Identify Project Requirements	The first step in determining the scope of a project is requirements identification. Here the project managers obtain first hand information on the requirements from the stakeholders. Once the requirements are clearly stated, they are evaluated and then further validated against resource availability, business needs, internal contingency, and other factors that influence the scope of the project.
Step 2: Define Project Objectives	In this stage, the stakeholders will define what should be the outcome of the project. Objectives are clearly laid down so that they can be monitored and assessed at every level of the project life cycle.
Step 3: Create Scope Statement	The project scope statement will be defined at this stage. Some of the essential criteria included in a project scope statement are: • Details of contract • Project objectives and requirements • Scope of the project • Project timeline • Project milestones and deliverables • Cost estimation • Compensation and payment • Roles and responsibilities of the people involved in the project • Terms and conditions, if any • Signature block

Stage	Description
Step 4: Scope Sign-off	In this stage, the scope statement is sent to all the stakeholders, sponsors, and contractors for an official approval, where the scope statement is read in its entirety by all the parties involved and then signed by all parties.

Project Charter

The project charter is a document that provides a clear and concise description of the business needs that the project is intended to address. It makes a project official; it authorizes the project manager to lead the project and draw on organizational resources as needed. The project charter documents initial assumptions about the project, any known constraints, and the expected results of the project.

Statement of Work

A Statement Of Work (SOW) is a document that describes the products or services that a project will supply. It specifies the work that will be done during the project and defines the business need that it is designed to meet. The SOW describes the product or service requirements and characteristics as well as the project scope and strategic plan. In addition, this document specifies the relationship between the business need and the product or service being created or provided to meet that need.

While the SOW describes everything from the beginning to the end of a planned work, the project charter only describes the tasks involved in a particular aspect of a job. For instance, consider an advertising agency whose core competence lies in content creation for billboards. While the agency uses its staff for creating content for a billboard, it may also procure contracts from external sources for some of the work considered necessary but are beyond its core capabilities, such as specialized printing and professional photography services. The project manager is required to create a SOW specifying how the management will get the overall work done and also to create project charters for each of the tasks outsourced.

How to Create a Project Scope Statement

An effective scope statement provides a high-level definition of a project and a basis for project stakeholders to make future decisions about the project's scope.

Guidelines

To create an effective project scope statement, follow these guidelines:

- Justify the need for the project.
- Clearly and concisely describe the critical characteristics and functionality of the project's product or service and the approach the team will take to achieve the project goals.
  - Ask questions to key stakeholders and customers to determine the required outcome.
  - Determine the critical characteristics of the product or service.
  - Conduct product analysis activities to develop a detailed view of the end result of the product or service.
  - Conduct alternative identification activities to generate alternative ways to achieve the project goals.

- Identify and list all the project's major deliverables whose full and satisfactory delivery constitutes completion of the project.
    - Conduct brainstorming sessions to determine the major deliverables of the product or service of the project.
    - Consult subject matter experts to identify what it will take to complete the project.
    - Consult organizational policies, relevant historical information, and the project sponsor or customer to determine which project management deliverables are required.
- Identify if there are any known exclusions to the project scope. These excluded activities are considered out of scope.
- Evaluate and validate or modify the constraints and assumptions made during initiation.
- Develop one or more project objectives—the quantifiable criteria that must be met for the project to be considered successful.
- Use precise and unambiguous language.
    - Write the project scope statement in user language rather than technical language.
    - If technical terms must be used, make sure they are clearly defined to avoid misunderstandings later.
- Ensure that all key project stakeholders receive a copy of the scope statement for review.
- Reexamine the project requirements if they need to be re-prioritized with respect to the results of the stakeholder analysis.
- Refine the project objectives, deliverables, and product scope description from the initial scope statement.
- Include a revised overall cost estimate and define any cost limitations.
- Create schedule milestones so that the client and the project team have dates for setting goals and measuring progress.
- Obtain consensus and formal approval from all key project stakeholders.

Example: Project Scope Statement Creation at OGC Office Products

OGC Office Products, has approached Carolyn, the project manager, with a request to determine the most cost-effective mode of transporting finished goods from China to the US. Carolyn determined the key requirements for the project in discussion with the stakeholders and outlined those requirements in the scope statement. She listed the criteria that could essentially mean successful completion of the project and also the terms that would not be included in the project. She then sends the scope statement to all stakeholders for approval and updates and makes it final based on their feedback.

Common Project Problems

Problems faced during a project can derail its progress. Common project problems stem from poorly understood success criteria, which should be established and shared during the initial stages of the project so that they do not arise in the later stages of the project when the cost of corrective action is high. The typical problems faced in any project are:

- Uncontrolled changes in the scope of the project
- Misunderstood deliverables
- Overworked or underworked resources
- Inappropriate schedules or budgets
- Dissatisfied customers or stakeholders

DISCOVERY ACTIVITY 2-1
Examining a Project Scope Statement

Scenario:

The scope statement for the Italian cookbook scenario is, "Create an Italian cookbook based on Mme. Tosca's favorite Southern Italian recipes that are suitable to be served at dinner. This includes appetizers, main dishes, pastas, and desserts." The upper limit for development cost is $200,000. Mme. Tosca's compensation, which includes an advance payment and royalties, is not included in that amount. The book must have at least 100 recipes, at least 20 attractive full-page color photos, lots of white space for making notes, and a picture of Mme. Tosca on the cover. It cannot be more than 200 pages long.

1. **Which are out of scope for the Italian cookbook project?**
    a) A recipe for Fettucine Alfredo, Mme. Tosca's favorite Northern Italian pasta.
    b) Recipes for Southern Italian dishes that Mme. Tosca served at dinner parties she catered for visiting dignitaries.
    c) The traditional breakfast food of Southern Italy.
    d) The traditional breakfast food of Northern Italy.

2. **Which is not a constraint to the cookbook project?**
    a) Start and end date of the project
    b) Schedule milestones
    c) Budget allotted to the project
    d) Page limit set for the book

3. **True or False? Things that limit the handling of a project are called constraints?**
    ___ True
    ___ False

4. **True or False? Objectives of a project need not necessarily be measurable.**
    ___ True
    ___ False

5. **Which should not be captured while examining the scope of the project?**
    a) Project assumptions
    b) The ways in which the project team will accomplish its objectives
    c) The benefits that the project will have for the organization
    d) Project constraints

TOPIC B
Identify the Skills for a Project Team

You outlined a well-defined scope statement and also identified the risk factors in a project. Your next step is to start the project with a team that befits the project objectives, which will in turn help you to form the ideal team to accomplish the goals of the project. In this topic, you will identify the skills for a project team.

People make projects happen. You may be well-versed in many aspects of project management, but you're not going to succeed if you can't put the right players on your team. Identifying the skillsets of the team members will increase your chances in finding the best possible people for your project.

Project Team

Definition:
A *project team* is a group of individuals who collectively have the skills required to complete a project. Every member of the project team possesses distinct skillsets and contributes collectively through the life of the project to achieve a common goal. The members of a project team may belong to different functional teams. The project team is headed by a project manager who is often selected by the stakeholders. Usually, project teams work together only for a defined period.

Example: A Marketing Team
Susan Williams is a project manager in an insurance company. She is responsible for marketing a wide range of new insurance schemes. She identifies the skills required for her team and decides that she needs a market specialist, designers for preparing presentations and hand bills, and a few volunteers to help her distribute pamphlets and answer customer queries.

Virtual Project Team
Project teams need not necessarily be located in the same geographical area. They can be scattered in different locations but still be a part of the project team by communicating through tools such as the phone, instant messaging, online meeting, and Voice over Internet connections. The primary reasons for forming virtual teams are organizational expectations and personal flexibility of the team members. However, there may be other reasons. Some of the key qualities required of a virtual project team are:

- Knowledge of the team members.
- Trust and respect for the team members.
- Ability to communicate effectively with the team members.
- Willingness to share project status information with the team members through email or phone regularly or periodically.

A virtual team is prone to risks such as lack of proper interaction between the team members, time zone differences, misinterpretation due to differences in language, and technological incompatibility.

Project Team Members

The members of a project team include core team members and implementation team members. The core team members are key individuals who work on the major activities that the team will undertake during the project, whereas, the implementation team members are individuals who carry out activities planned by the core team members. The members of the project team grow during the implementation phase of the project. Some of the implementation team members stay with the team for a short span of time, while others stay throughout the entire implementation phase. The core team members stay throughout the life of a project.

Team Skills Matrix

The team skills matrix helps you to identify the team members you need, to perform the tasks in a project. It includes a listing of the skills required to complete the project tasks and the level of skill required to accomplish those tasks. In addition, it includes a list of selection criteria that helps you determine whether team members possess those skills. Based on the skill requirements matching, you can select the members for the project team. A meticulously prepared skills matrix helps you in the selection of team members or in the identification of missing skills in the current team.

Team Skills Matrix Selection Criteria					
Skills	Skills Level Required for the job	Supervision Required for the job	Experience Level Required for the job	Education Level Required for the job	Team Member
Cooking	Main dishes, sauces Familiar with Italian ingredients Can convert from Italian to US metrics	Ability to work unsupervised but willing to work under direction of Mme Tosca Willing to work from recipes	Minimum 3 years as restaurant head chef; small restaurant experience desirable	Culinary School certificate desirable but not required	Warren Scarpia
Writing	Procedural (recipe) writing Interviewing Editing	Unsupervised	Minimum 5 years technical writing, at least 3 cookbook projects	B.A.	Jane Walker
Assisting in kitchen (cooking)	Stirring Basting Making pasta Chopping vegetables	Supervised		Minimum 1 year professional kitchen experience	Andrea Ben

Figure 2-2: Skills matrix for the cookbook project.

How to Identify the Skills for a Project Team

Procedure Reference: Identify the Skills for a Project Team

To identify the skills for a project team:

1. List down the objectives of the project.
2. Against each project objective, brainstorm a list of skills required to accomplish the objective.
3. Beside each skill, specify the criteria that you would use to measure whether someone has met the skill requirement. The criteria can include the amount of supervision required for the job, the amount or level of experience required, and the education level required.
4. Match the skills and criteria against the credentials of the core team members.
5. If a team member meets the requirement, specify his or her name in the corresponding box in the right-hand column. The blank spaces in the right-hand column indicate that the team lacks the required skills.

DISCOVERY ACTIVITY 2-2
Identifying Skills Using the Skills Matrix

Scenario:
The team skills matrix for the Italian cookbook project is ready. You now need to determine how to handle the resource requirements for the project.

Skills	Skill level required for the job	Supervision required for the job	Experience level required for the job	Education level required for the job	Team member
Cooking	Main dishes, sauces. Familiarity with Italian ingredients. Can convert from Italian to the US metrics.	Ability to work unsupervised but willing to work under direction of Mme Tosca. Willing to work with the recipes.	Minimum 3 years as restaurant head chef; small restaurant experience desirable.	Culinary school certificate desirable but not required.	Warren Scarpia
Baking	Italian-style pastry and cakes. Familiarity with Italian ingredients. Can convert from Italian to the US metrics.	Ability to work unsupervised but willing to work under the direction of Mme Tosca. Willing to work with the recipes.	Minimum 3 years as pastry chef; small restaurant or bakery experience desirable.	Culinary school certificate desirable but not required.	Sandra Oldenberg
Assisting in kitchen (cooking)	Stirring, basting, making soda, chopping vegetables, grinding meats, washing dishes.	Supervised	Minimum 1 year professional kitchen experience.		Andrea Ben
Assisting in kitchen (baking)	Whipping cream, chopping fruits, shaving chocolate, mixing pastry dough, washing pans. Have minimal experience in cooking.	Supervised	Minimum 1 year professional kitchen experience.		Carl Cavarradossi
Writing	Procedural recipe writing. Interviewing, editing.	Unsupervised	Minimum 5 years technical writing, at least 3 cook book projects	B.A.	Jane Walker
Photography	Thorough understanding of camera operation. Experience in digital photography.	Unsupervised	Minimum 3 years of experience in photography		

1. If you were the project manager for the Italian cookbook project, how will you respond to the blank spaces?

2. Warren Scarpia is not in a position to continue in the team due to unavoidable circumstances. The management is now contemplating the right person to take his position and complete the tasks. Who do you think will be the right person to replace Warren Scarpia?

    a) Jane Walker

    b) Carl Cavarradossi

    c) Sandra Oldenberg

    d) Andrea Ben

3. True or False? Recruiting people with the competencies listed against the empty team member spaces in the team skills matrix will help fill the empty spaces in the matrix.

    ___ True

    ___ False

4. Which team member can assist in both cooking and baking when under supervision?

    a) Sandra Oldenberg

    b) Carl Cavarradossi

    c) Jane Walker

    d) Andrea Ben

5. What are the uses of a team skills matrix?

    a) Identify the availability of team members.

    b) Identify which team members have the required skillsets.

    c) Break out skills needed for each project task.

    d) Identify criteria that may be used to determine whether a team member has a particular skillset.

TOPIC C
Identify the Risks to a Project

You took considerable effort to determine the scope of the project so that you can get the project started. You now need to spot and tackle the problems which may arise during the course of your project. In this topic, you will identify the risks involved in a project.

Unexpected events can upset your work plan or bring your project to a halt. Identifying risks early helps you to reduce their severity. Risk identifying allows you to be proactive in your approach towards problems, rather than scrambling to respond to problems.

Risk

Definition:

A *risk* is an uncertain event that may have a positive or negative effect on a project. Its primary components are a measure of probability that a risk will occur and the impact of the risk on a project. In project management, the risk that matters is anything that might negatively impact the project's completion on time, within the defined scope and budget while conforming to the predefined quality standards.

Example: Risks in a Project Involving Production of Promotional Materials

Sheila, a bank manager, is acting as a project manager, overseeing the production of new promotional materials for her bank's mortgage division. Sheila hires independent contractors, including a graphic designer, copywriter, and commercial printer. She wants the materials produced soon, but she recognizes that the risks include increased costs in rush printing fees and a greater probability of errors because the job is being pushed quickly through its production cycle.

Impact of Risk Over Time

Project risks progress over time. The probability of risk over an event is minimal during the initial stage of a project, therefore risk controlled effectively during this stage can prove to be cost-effective. The impact of risk over time multiplies as the project progresses, wherefore the possibility of meeting the project's planned scope, time, and budget becomes arduous.

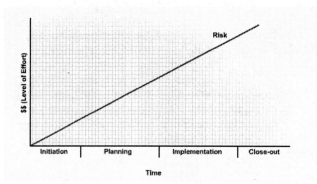

Figure 2-3: Progression of risk over time.

How to Identify the Risks to a Project

Identifying and documenting risks helps you plan for risks that might affect the project development.

Guidelines

To identify project risks, follow these guidelines:

- Determine the potential people risks associated with a project.
    - Will team members be available when needed?
    - Do they understand the project's purpose and objectives?
    - Can they work together?
- Determine the technology based risk associated with the project.
    - Does the team have the right skills?
    - Are the tools and software available appropriate? robust? scalable?
- Determine the organization based risk associated with the project.
    - Do all stakeholders agree on project objectives and purpose?
    - Are there stakeholders who have not participated in initiating the project?
    - Does the sponsor have enough clout to influence other stakeholders?
- Determine the finance based risk associated with the project.
    - Will the project manager require multiple sign-offs before spending money? If so, how much time will they take and what is the scheduling impact?
    - Will currency fluctuations impact availability of cash?
    - Does ongoing funding depend on the timeliness of the client's progress payments?
- Determine the Law or Contract-based risk associated with the project.
    - Are pending regulatory issues likely to impact project specifications?
    - Do suppliers own the patent for the technology you expect to purchase?

- Determine the physical risk associated with the project.
  - Are workers more likely to get hurt if you increase the number of hours they work?
  - Has your company undertaken fire prevention measures?
- Determine the environment risks associated with the project.
  - How will an early hurricane season impact the project?
  - Will environmental pollution impact the clean room air quality?
  - Will municipal construction projects impact the productivity?
- Lookout for special circumstances that might arise in any project segment.
- Consult relevant historical information from previous, similar projects that may include lessons learned describing problems and their resolutions.

Example: Identification of Risks in a Construction Project

For a project involving the construction of a commercial establishment, news of an impending construction workers' strike will be a risk. If the construction work on the project is not complete, the risk will have a negative effect on the project and it will delay the completion of the project. If the construction work is complete, the risk will have a positive effect on the company's goodwill as the project was completed on time despite the strike.

DISCOVERY ACTIVITY 2-3
Identifying Sources of Risk

Scenario:
Based on what you know so far about the Italian cookbook project, brainstorm some potential sources of risk.

1. **What do you think are some of the potential risks for the cookbook project?**
    a) Behavior of the team members
    b) Availability of Mme. Tosca
    c) Paper quality of the cookbook
    d) Availability of adequate kitchen facilities for cooking and testing recipes

2. **Under which risk type will you categorize the risk of unavailability of Mme. Tosca?**
    a) Physical
    b) Environment Risk
    c) People Risk
    d) Technology

3. **Under which risk type will you categorize the risk of stakeholders disagreeing to project goals and objectives?**
    a) Organizational
    b) Law or Contract
    c) Finance
    d) People

4. **True or False? The probability of risk over an event is maximum during the initial stages of a project.**
    ___ True
    ___ False

Lesson 2 Follow-up

In this lesson, you explored the significant elements of initiating a project, which is one of the primary processes and a critical part of every project. By effectively initiating a project and laying a solid foundation for the work that will follow, you will significantly increase your chances for success.

1. **Consider the benefits of developing a project scope statement. How do you anticipate using this process to your advantage in your next project?**

2. **What do you think is the significance of risk identification and what lessons on risk identification will you offer to others?**

3 | Planning for Time and Cost

Lesson Time: 1 hour(s), 15 minutes

Lesson Objectives:

In this lesson, you will plan for time and cost.

You will:

- Create a Work Breakdown Structure (WBS).
- Sequence the activities.
- Create a project schedule.
- Determine project costs.

Introduction

You initiated a project and identified the skills required to perform the project tasks. Now that you have a solid foundation to start the project, you need to plan for its successful completion. In this lesson, you will plan for the project time and cost.

The ability to deliver projects on time and within budget is the cornerstone of good project management. By identifying the methods of creating accurate duration, resources, and cost estimates that will guide your projects, you can meet the expectations and deliver the desired results.

TOPIC A
Create a Work Breakdown Structure

You created a project scope statement and identified the skills required for the project team. The next logical step will be to identify the smaller tasks in the project that can be assigned to the individual team members. In this topic, you will create a work breakdown structure.

It's always easier to successfully complete a project by breaking it down into smaller, more manageable chunks. Creating an effective work breakdown structure helps you schedule the project work and create accurate time, cost, and resource estimates.

WBS

Definition:

The Work Breakdown Structure *(WBS)* is a hierarchical structure that subdivides project work into smaller, more manageable pieces of work. The work defined in the WBS maps to the project's scope statement, and it has to be executed by the project team to accomplish the project objectives. A WBS helps to identify project deliverables. It provides an increasingly detailed definition of the project work at each descending level, with the lowest-level components, called work packages, containing components of work that can be scheduled, cost estimated, monitored, and controlled. The level of detail of the work packages will vary depending on the size and complexity of the project.

Example: Work Breakdown Structure

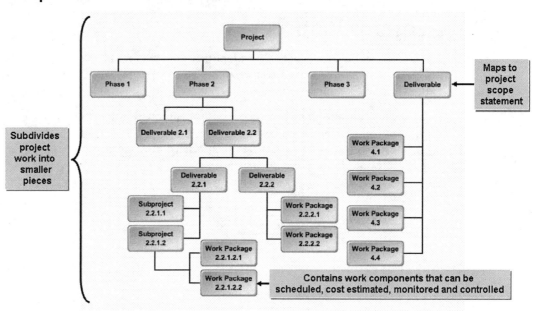

Helps to identify deliverables

Decomposition

Decomposition is a technique for creating the WBS by subdividing project work to the work package level. An analysis of the scope statement will help to identify the project work. The level of decomposition varies for different projects. Decomposition of a project work is stopped when the components of the work packages are sufficient to complete the work and can be assigned to an individual, cost estimated, scheduled, and monitored.

How to Create a Work Breakdown Structure

Procedure Reference: Develop a Work Breakdown Structure (WBS)

To develop a WBS:

1. Gather the reference materials and other inputs you will need. Some of the materials needed include:
   - The scope statement.
   - A WBS template, if available.
   - Constraints and assumptions.
   - Relevant historical information.
   - Other planning inputs that may impact scope definition.

2. Determine how you are going to organize the work of your project. Organizational options include organizing by:
   - Major product deliverables.
   - Life cycle phases.
   - Organizational or functional responsibility.
   - Geographical location.

   Regardless of the organization, these elements represent the level directly below the project name on your WBS.

3. Identify the major work, or subprojects, for the project.

4. Decompose the major work or subprojects.

5. Analyze each element to determine whether it is sufficiently decomposed.
   - Can each element be assigned to an individual person or group?
   - Can each element be adequately scheduled and budgeted?

6. If necessary, continue to break down each WBS element into subdeliverables until you reach the work package level.

7. Validate your WBS using a bottom-up approach.
    - Determine if the lower-level components are necessary and sufficient for the completion of each decomposed item.
    - Ensure that each element is described as a deliverable (preferably as a noun), and is distinguishable from all other deliverables.
    - Determine if each element can be adequately budgeted, scheduled, and assigned to an individual person or group.
    - A disproportionate number of levels may indicate that the deliverable is inappropriately decomposed. Analyze the element to determine whether one of the higher level components should be broken into two subdeliverables or whether two or more subdeliverables should be combined.
8. If necessary, make the desired modifications.

DISCOVERY ACTIVITY 3-1
Creating a Work Breakdown Structure

Scenario:
The Italian cookbook team is expected to create a first draft of the book. The first draft will include a write up of the recipes and some anecdotes. You now want to create a WBS for this task.

1. **As a project manager, you are asked to decompose the "First draft" subproject. What is the task you would be doing?**
    a) Assign cost values to each deliverable.
    b) Arrange the deliverables into categories, based on risk.
    c) Breakdown the deliverables of the subproject into smaller components.
    d) Organize deliverables based on which team is responsible for their completion.

2. **What WBS components will you obtain after the first level of decomposition of the "First draft" subproject?**
    a) Shoot photos, obtain approval, and reshoot photos that require revisions.
    b) Create an attractive page layout and assemble the recipes.
    c) Create recipes and write anecdotes.
    d) Test recipes and edit them.

3. **Which components will make up the next level of decomposition of the "Create recipes" component?**
    a) Write up recipes using US metrics.
    b) Test recipes for accuracy and taste.
    c) Revise recipes.
    d) Write notes about the exotic ingredients used in the recipes.

4. **Which components will make up the next level of decomposition of the "Write anecdote text" component?**
    a) Collect anecdotes.
    b) Write up anecdotes.
    c) Incorporate Francesca Tosca's revisions to the anecdotes.
    d) Write up a page about Francesca Tosca and her reputation.

TOPIC B
Sequence the Activities

You have created a work breakdown structure and identified the activities in a project. Before you begin to develop a project plan for scheduling the activities, you need to identify the order in which the individual activities need to be performed. In this topic, you will sequence the activities.

Identifying the activities in a project and the relationships between them is a fundamental step for determining the order in which the activities need to be performed. Careful sequencing of the activities will ensure that the project progresses towards its successful completion.

Activity

Definition:

An *activity* is a unit of project work that must be performed to complete a project deliverable. Every activity has a duration and cost, and consumes resources. Activities occur at the lowest level of the work breakdown structure. An activity takes inputs to perform the work required and produces outputs that may serve as inputs to another activity. Activities differ in the complexity of work involved, the duration required to complete them, the resources they require, the cost involved, the outputs they produce, and their criticality to successful project completion.

Activity Sequencing

Activity sequencing involves identifying and documenting the relationships among activities, and arranging the activities in a sequence based on those relationships. Identification of relationships helps to determine the correct order in which the activities need to be performed. A correct sequence of activities is essential for the development of an achievable project plan. Activity sequencing can be carried out using project management software, manual techniques, or a combination of both.

Dependencies

An *activity dependency* is a logical relationship between two activities that indicates whether the start of one activity depends upon an event or input from another activity or an external factor. There are three types of dependencies.

Type	*Description*
Mandatory	A mandatory dependency is inherent in the nature of the project work. Activities are supposed to have a mandatory dependency if they have to be performed in a particular sequence for the work to be completed successfully.
	Example: Books can't be bound before they're printed.

Type	Description
Discretionary	A discretionary dependency is established by the project manager if there are no mandatory or external dependencies between the activities. The project manager applies the application area's best practices and uses his previous experience to decide on the sequence of the activities. **Example:** The sponsor would like to see the book's cover design as soon as possible, so the team may decide to have the cover artwork done before the inside illustrations.
External	An external dependency is an event or input outside the project activities that dictates the sequence of the activities. **Example:** Books can't be printed until the shipment of paper arrives.

Precedence Relationships

A *precedence relationship* is a logical relationship between two activities that indicates which activity should be performed first and which one should be performed later. The activity that is performed first is called the predecessor activity, and the one that is performed later is called the successor activity.

There are four types of precedence relationships.

Type	Description
Finish-to-Start	The precedence relationship in which the predecessor activity must finish before the successor activity can start. **Example:** The foundation for the house must be finished (Activity A) before the framing can start (Activity B).
Finish-to-Finish	The precedence relationship in which the predecessor activity must finish before the successor activity can finish. **Example:** Construction must be finished (Activity A) before the building inspection can be finished (Activity B).
Start-to-Start	The precedence relationship in which the predecessor activity must start before the successor activity can start. **Example:** The building design must start (Activity A) before the electrical layout design can start (Activity B).

Type	Description
Start-to-Finish	The precedence relationship in which the predecessor activity must start before the successor activity can finish. **Example:** The electrical inspections must start (Activity A) before you can finish the drywalling (Activity B).

Project Schedule Network Diagrams

A *project schedule network diagram* is a graphical representation of the activities in a project and the logical relationships between those activities. There are two methods for constructing a project schedule network diagram. The Precedence Diagramming Method (PDM) is a technique for creating a project schedule network diagram in which activities are represented by boxes or rectangles, referred to as nodes, and relationships are represented by arrows connecting the nodes. The Arrow Diagramming Method (ADM) is a technique for creating a project schedule network diagram in which activities are represented by arrows, and their relationships are represented by connecting the arrows using nodes.

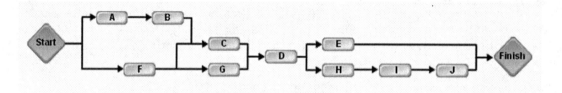

Figure 3-1: A precedence diagram.

Lag

A *lag* is a modification in a logical relationship that delays the start of a successor activity. It is determined by an external or mandatory dependency and may affect activities with any of the four precedence relationships. Lag time is considered a positive value since it adds time to the overall duration of a project.

Lead

A *lead* is a modification in a logical relationship that allows the successor activity to start before the predecessor activity ends in a Finish-to-Start relationship. A lead is implemented when you need to accelerate a successor activity in order to shorten the overall project schedule. Lead time is considered a negative value since it lessens the overall duration of a project.

How to Sequence the Activities
Procedure Reference: How to Create a PDM Project Schedule Network Diagram

To create a PDM project schedule network diagram:
1. Determine the dependencies among project activities.
2. Identify the predecessor and successor activities.
   a. Create a table with two columns.
   b. In the first column, list each activity to be sequenced. Identify each with a letter.
   c. In the second column, write the letter of the predecessor activities for each activity.
3. Create nodes for all activities with no predecessor activities or dependencies.
4. Create nodes for all activities that are successor activities to the nodes already created.
5. Draw arrows from the predecessor activities to the successor activities.
6. Continue drawing the network diagram, working from left to right until all activities are included on the diagram and their precedence relationships are indicated by arrows.
7. Verify the accuracy of your diagram. Check to ensure that:
   a. All activities are included in the diagram.
   b. All precedence relationships are correctly indicated by arrows going from the predecessor activities to the successor activities.
   c. Any known lags or leads are indicated in the diagram.

ACTIVITY 3-2
Sequencing Activities in a Project Schedule Network Diagram

Scenario:
You identified the activities in a project and determined the logical relationships that exist between them. You realize that a Finish-to-Start precedence relationship exists between the activities in the project. Using these inputs, you have come up with a project schedule network diagram. You need to check whether you have got the activities in the correct sequence and add two tasks to the diagram.

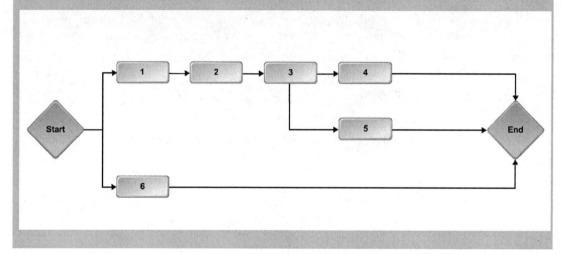

What You Do	How You Do It

1. You need to add an additional Task 7 to the network diagram. Task 7 must not begin until Task 6 is complete and Task 5 is dependent on Task 7. Which would be the most appropriate location for this task in the network diagram? Sketch your answer.

2. You need to add an additional Task 8 to the network diagram. Task 8 does not begin until tasks 4 and 5 are complete. Which would be the most appropriate location for this task in the network diagram? Sketch your answer.

3. According to the project schedule network diagram, which is Task 3's predecessor activity?

   a) Task 5
   b) Task 6
   c) Task 2
   d) Task 4

Lesson 3: Planning for Time and Cost   49

4. **What task can be done in parallel with Task 1?**
   a) Task 4
   b) Task 3
   c) Task 6
   d) Task 2

TOPIC C
Create a Project Schedule

You sequenced the activities in a project. The next step is to develop a project plan for performing these activities. In this topic, you will create a project schedule.

Given the importance of the project schedule and its high visibility, you want to make sure that the schedule you create is realistic. To arrive at a project schedule that is achievable, it is important to estimate the resource availability and establish realistic start and finish dates for each activity.

Resource Estimation

Resource estimation is the means of determining the resources required to complete project activities. Resources refer to any useful material object or any person needed for the project work to be completed. Resource estimates specify the quantities of the resources that will be used and the period for which the resources should be available to perform the activities. Resources are almost always limited in quantity and therefore require thoughtful allocation.

Resource Leveling

Resource leveling is a technique that assists in making scheduling decisions when there are resource management concerns. It allows you to readjust the work as appropriate so that people are not overly allocated. It is also used to address scheduling activities when critical resources are only available at certain times.

Duration Estimation

Duration estimation is the act of estimating the time periods that are required to complete project activities. To estimate durations, the scope of work of an activity, the required resources, the time periods for which the resources will be required, and the availability of resources during those time periods are taken into account. The duration estimation process calculates the amount of effort and the amount of resources required to arrive at an estimate of the time required to complete each activity. Duration estimation is performed by the project manager in consultation with the project team members who are familiar with the nature of the work to be performed.

Schedule Baseline

The schedule baseline is the version of the project schedule that is approved by stakeholders and serves as the basis for measuring the project's progress. It contains the planned start and finish dates for all the activities.

Schedule Development Terminologies

The schedule development terms are used to identify the key parameters of a project schedule.

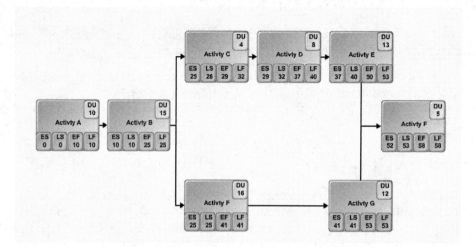

Figure 3-2: *A precedence diagram showing values for the schedule development terms.*

Term	Description
DU	Duration. The number of work periods required for the completion of an activity.
ES	Early start. The earliest time an activity can start. The ES of the first activity in a network diagram is zero. The ES of all other activities is the latest early finish (EF) of any predecessor activities (assuming that any successor activity starts as soon as all its predecessor activities are finished).
EF	Early finish. The earliest time an activity can finish. The EF for the first activity is the same as its duration. For all other activities, EF is the latest EF of all of an activity's predecessor activities plus its duration.
LF	Late finish. The latest time an activity can finish. The LF for the last activity is the same as its EF time. The LF for any predecessor activity is the earliest LS of any of its successor activities.
LS	Late start. The latest time an activity can start. The LS for the last activity is its EF minus its duration. The LS for any predecessor activity is its LF minus its duration.

Critical Path

Definition:
Critical path is the path in the project schedule network diagram that has the longest duration. The duration of the critical path is calculated by adding the durations of the individual activities along the path. Activities on the critical path cannot be delayed as it will delay the whole project, unless the subsequent activities are shortened.

Example: Critical Path

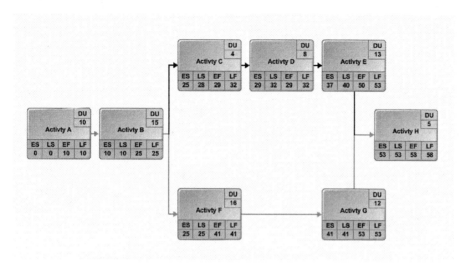

Float

Float is the amount of time an activity can be delayed without delaying the ES of the immediate successor activity. *Total float* is the amount of time an activity can be delayed from its ES without delaying the project finish date. It is calculated by subtracting an activity's EF from its LF or its ES from its LS. In most cases, float has a value greater than zero only in activities that are not on the critical path. If there are two or more activities in a path with float, the total float for that string of activities is shared by all the activities in the string. If one activity uses all of the float, there's none left for the others. Float is also called free float or slack.

How to Create a Project Schedule

Procedure Reference: Creating a Project Schedule

To create a project schedule:

1. Perform an analysis to determine the period within which activities could be scheduled once resource limits and other known constraints are applied.
2. Evaluate the possible impact of any constraints and assumptions on schedule development.
3. Consider the availability of your resources.
   - Will you have the staff you need to perform the work when it is scheduled to be done?
   - Will you have access to the materials, facilities, and equipment you need to perform the work when it is scheduled to be done?
4. Consult project calendars and assign dates to activities.
   - Are there any holidays during which your project team will not conduct work activities?
   - Will your project team conduct work activities on weekends?
   - When will your key project team members be taking vacations?
   - Are there any unmovable milestone dates that must be met?
5. Consider external resource date constraints, if applicable.
   - Are there any regional or national holidays not previously accounted for?
   - Do you need to make considerations for travel time for meetings?
6. Select project management software that best meets the needs and budget of your project. If your organization does not require the use of a particular software program, ask yourself the following questions to make the selection:
   - How complex is the project?
   - Do I need to manage more than one project at a time?
   - How easy will the software be to learn and to use?
   - How well will the software adapt to projects that vary greatly?
   - What type and depth of analyses do I need to perform?
   - What is the reputation of the software company?
   - What do other project managers in the field use and what do they recommend?
7. Review rough drafts of the schedule with the project team, sponsor, and customer. You may also need to review the rough drafts with functional managers to ensure that there are no conflicts with functional resources.
8. Distribute the preliminary schedule to all program office personnel, functional team members, functional management, and the customer or sponsor to obtain approval.

ACTIVITY 3-3
Creating a Project Schedule

Scenario:
You have identified the proper sequence of the project activities and completed the project schedule network diagram. You have also estimated the duration of each activity. You need to identify the activities in the project that cannot be delayed and find out the early start, early finish, late start, and late finish values of all the activities in the project.

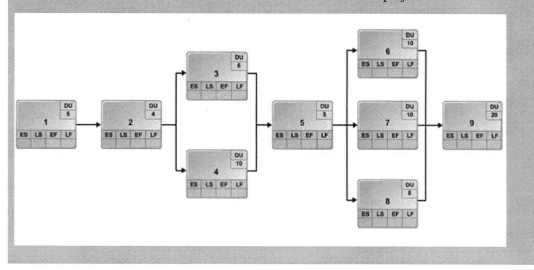

What You Do	How You Do It

1. In the given project schedule, the ES value of Task 1 is 0 and duration is 5. What will be the calculated EF value of Task 1? Sketch your answer in the diagram provided.

Lesson 3: Planning for Time and Cost

2. What will be the early start value of Task 2?

3. Calculate the early finish value of Task 2, given the early start value is 5 and duration is 4.

4. Consider the early finish value of Task 2 as 9, the duration of Task 3 as 6, and the duration of Task 4 as 10. What will be the early start and early finish values of tasks 3 and 4?

5. What will be the early start and early finish values for Task 5?

6. What are the early start and early finish values of tasks 6, 7, 8, and 9?

7. For Task 9, the early start value is 34 and early finish value is 54. What will be the calculated late finish value of Task 9?

8. The late finish value of Task 9 is 54. What is the late start value of Task 9?

9. What are the late finish and late start values of Task 8?

10. What are the late finish and late start values for tasks 6 and 7?

11. What are the late finish and late start values for Task 5?

12. What are the late finish and late start values for tasks 1, 2, 3, and 4?

13. Which is the critical path for this project?
    a) 1, 2, 4, 5, 8, 9
    b) 1, 2, 3, 5, 6, 9
    c) 1, 2, 4, 5, 6, 9
    d) 1, 2, 3, 5, 8, 9

14. What is the duration of the critical path?
    a) 54
    b) 56
    c) 52
    d) 50

15. Which activities in the project do not fall on the critical path?
    a) Task 6
    b) Task 4
    c) Task 3
    d) Task 8

TOPIC D
Determine Project Costs

You have drafted a project schedule. To arrive at an estimate of how much your project is going to cost, you need to calculate the cost involved in performing each activity in the schedule. In this topic, you will estimate project costs.

Inappropriately high cost estimates may discourage sponsors from pursuing projects that have the potential for success. Conversely, estimates that are too low could waste precious resources on a project that ultimately proves unfeasible. As a project manager, it is your responsibility to estimate project costs as accurately as possible.

Cost Estimates

A *cost estimate* is an assessment of the likely costs of the resources required to complete an activity. It also involves identifying risks that might affect the cost required to perform the activities. It is expressed in monetary values. Historical cost information of similar projects can help a project manager in estimating costs. The accuracy of cost estimates increases as the project progresses.

Cost Budgeting

Cost budgeting is the process of aggregating the cost estimates of all the activities or work packages to arrive at an overall cost estimate for the project. Cost budgeting also takes contract information of resources, project constraints, and risks into account while arriving at an estimate for the project. The outcome of cost budgeting serves as the foundation for monitoring project costs as the project progresses. It also serves to find out if the project will require additional funding and helps stakeholders assess the financial feasibility of the project.

Cost Baseline

The cost baseline is an outcome of cost budgeting that is approved by stakeholders and serves as the basis for measuring the project's progress. It contains a summation of the estimated costs of the activities by period.

How to Determine Project Costs

Accurately estimating project costs will prevent overruns and unforeseen expenditure.

Guidelines

To develop accurate cost estimates, follow these guidelines:

- Involve the work package owners.
  - When possible, the cost figures that go into the cost estimates for individual work packages should be provided by those who will actually provide the resources. As always, it is the people who will do the work, provide the service, or supply the material that can best estimate what the associated costs will be. It is the project manager's responsibility to compile these cost figures into realistic estimates.
  - For some projects, though, the project manager will be solely responsible for generating the cost estimates. This may be the case for:
    - Small projects in which the project manager is very familiar with the activities required.
    - Projects with very well-defined resource requirements.
    - Projects that are very similar to past projects for which the costs are well documented. Even in such cases, the project manager may want to do a quick reality check with the resource supplier to make sure no incorrect assumptions have been made.
- Gather any relevant input information that may help you prepare the estimates, such as estimating publications and resource rates.
- Look for alternative costing options. Some options you might explore could include:
  - Using stock components versus custom-made.
  - Stretching the duration of an activity to eliminate overtime charges.
  - Leasing versus purchase of capital equipment.
  - Outsourcing as opposed to handling the work inhouse.
- Determine the units of measure that will be used.
  - Estimates should all be in the same unit of measure (usually monetary).
  - Units must be clearly defined and easily interpreted.
- Consider possible risks that may impact cost.
- Ensure that all cost estimates are assigned to the appropriate account, according to the chart of accounts.
- Make sure your cost estimates include the following key elements:
  - Estimated costs for all resources that will be charged to the project. Use the WBS and resource requirements document to develop the estimates.
  - The level of estimate.
  - A list of assumptions made when developing the estimates.

Example:

While estimating the costs of a research project, you discuss with the research team and arrive at rough estimates for the work packages. You also determine the rates for the resources involved in the project and the technologies they will use. You also weigh the costs of outsourcing the work in the project as opposed to doing it in-house. You then identify the availability of authentic information and appropriate technologies as possible risks to the project. Finally, you review the cost estimates and submit them along with a list of assumptions that you made while arriving at those estimates.

DISCOVERY ACTIVITY 3-4

Determining Project Costs

Scenario:
You have drafted a project schedule after sequencing the activities and estimating the resource and activity duration. Now, you need to find out the cost of the individual activities and that of the project as a whole.

1. **What information does the cost estimate of an activity in the project convey?**
   a) The cost incurred by the activity in a similar past project.
   b) The estimated cost of resources required to perform the activity.
   c) The project's budgeted cost.
   d) The pay received by each resource per hour.

2. **True or False? During the cost budgeting of the Italian cookbook project, you need to take Francesca Tosca's contract information into account.**
   __ True
   __ False

3. **Upon cost budgeting the Italian cookbook project, what important analyses can the stakeholders perform?**
   a) Assess the financial feasibility of the project.
   b) Determine market demand for the book.
   c) Determine additional funding requirements.
   d) Identify the risks to the project.

Lesson 3 Follow-up

In this lesson, you planned for project time and cost. Planning the time and cost of a project will help you meet expectations and deliver the desired results.

1. **How important is the WBS in creating an effective project schedule? What is the level of decomposition you will like to achieve in order to manage your project efficiently?**

2. **How will the ability to estimate costs effectively improve your performance on the job?**

4 Planning for Project Risks, Communication, and Change Control

Lesson Time: 30 minutes

Lesson Objectives:

In this lesson, you will plan for project risks, communication, and change control.

You will:

- Analyze the risks to a project.
- Create a communication plan.
- Plan for change control.

Introduction

You have planned the time and cost for the project. Now you may need to proceed with the other elements of good planning. In this lesson, you'll plan for project risks, communication, and change control in your project.

You want to make sure that none of the customers, stakeholders, or members of the project management team are surprised by delays, changes, or unavoidable risks. By planning ahead and monitoring the project, you can increase your chances of leading the project to a successful completion.

TOPIC A
Analyze the Risks to a Project

You are well aware of the potential risks that would affect your project. You now need to analyze them so that they can be mitigated. In this topic, you'll analyze the risks to a project.

The nature of project management has its inherent risks that things can go differently than you had hoped or planned for. Deciding how to approach a project risk early in the planning phase can help you to maximize the opportunities in positive risks and minimize the consequences of adverse risks that may occur during the life of a project.

Qualitative Analysis

Qualitative analysis is a method of assessing, ranking, and prioritizing risks for subsequent analysis. It takes into account the probability of different risks occurring and their likely impact. It is conducted early in the project life cycle so that potential problems can be identified early to develop an effective and favorable outcome. When qualitative analysis is repeated, trends can be evaluated and corrective action may be taken to avoid or lessen a negative consequence.

Quantitative Analysis

Quantitative analysis is a numerical method used to assess the impact of risk and to measure the amount of damage that can take place. Quantifying risk can help you to identify time and cost contingencies of a project and also to prioritize risks. Based on time and budget allotments the project manager performs quantitative analysis. It involves gathering documents indicating risk planning and project scope, analyzing each risk using risk management tools, and finally entering any alterations into account. Quantitative analysis further refines and enhances the prioritization and scoring produced during qualitative analysis.

Risk Response Plan

A risk response plan is a plan used to decrease the possibility or impact of risk in order to accomplish project objectives. You can create different types of plans to counter risks.

Risk Response Plan	Used To
Avoidance	Find a work-around so that the risk never occurs.
Acceptance	Decide to live with the consequences, should the risk occur.
Mitigation	Prepare to deal with the risk through contingency planning.
Transference	Get someone else to share the risk or underwrite it for you.

How to Analyze the Risks to a Project

Performing risk analysis enables the project team to prioritize risks according to the threat they pose or the opportunity they present to the project. The prioritized list can be used to develop an effective response plan for each risk.

Guidelines

To effectively perform risk analysis, follow these guidelines:

- Examine the list of identified risks and make sure that all the identified risks are documented.
- Include guidelines or requirements regarding the outset of the risk.
- Analyze the data available for each risk.
    - Does the source of the data fully understand the risk?
    - Is the source reliable and trustworthy?
    - Is the amount of data sufficient to adequately analyze the risk?
    - What is the accuracy and quality of the data?
    - Are there risks that require further monitoring?
- Analyze the assumptions identified during risk identification to determine the validity of the assumption and the impact on the project, if false.
- Analyze the probability and impact of each identified risk using well-defined probability and impact scales.
- Consult historical information, such as similar completed projects, studies of similar projects by risk specialists, and risk databases for information that may be useful for risk analysis on your project.
- Prioritize risks.
- Document all changes.

Example: Analyzing the Risks in a Research Project

One of the risks identified for the research project is the availability of authentic information. The project team, on analysis, determined that unavailability of information on subscribed sites could indicate the outset of this risk. You analyze the impact of this risk on the project and document the information for future analysis.

DISCOVERY ACTIVITY 4-1
Analyzing the Risks to a Project

Scenario:
You have identified the risks related to the cookbook project. You now need to plan for all risks associated with the project.

1. What would be your primary task while analyzing a risk?

    a) Assign roles and responsibilities to each team member.

    b) Develop response strategies.

    c) Create an organization chart.

    d) Coordinate risk identification and risk analysis activities.

2. Which of the risks should receive the highest priority for this project?

    a) Temporary loss of a team member.

    b) Stakeholders not agreeing to the objectives of the project.

    c) Incompatibility of team members.

    d) Currency fluctuations.

3. What factors should you consider while analyzing risks?

    a) Geography of the project

    b) Historical Information

    c) Probability of risk

    d) Job Description

    e) Source of risk

4. **Associate the risk response plans with the techniques used to arrive at it.**

___ The lead chef is known to have a heart condition. The publishers are concerned that their investment may be lost if the lead chef cannot complete the book due to health problems. They plan to buy a "key man" policy that insures them against loss if the lead chef becomes ill or dies.

a. Transference

___ The authors are concerned that readers may not be able to find authentic ingredients outside Italy. They plan to limit the ingredients to items that can be found in a typical U.S. supermarket.

b. Mitigation

___ The publishers are concerned that the cookbook will be too short. They plan to add additional photos, if the first draft seems too short by a few pages; if it is too short by 20 pages, they plan to add additional white space in the margins and increase the font size. If it is too short by more than 20 pages, they plan to resubmit it to the authors and request additional recipes.

c. Acceptance

___ The authors are concerned that new cooks may not know common cooking techniques like how to baste a roast or how to whip cream. They plan to assume that most of their readers are advanced-level cooks who will know how to perform these techniques.

d. Avoidance

TOPIC B
Create a Communication Plan

You analyzed risks using different risk analysis methods and planned to mitigate them or reduce their impact on project objectives. Now you may need to ensure that relevant information is available to stakeholders during the course of a project. In this topic, you'll create a communication plan.

An effective communication plan ensures that the right people receive the right information at the right time. You don't want your people expending unnecessary energy reporting on every little detail. Nor do you want to spend hours unnecessarily generating long reports. Mastering the tools and techniques to develop an effective communication management plan will ensure that you deliver the significant information to your stakeholders when they need it.

Communication Plan

Definition:

A *communication plan* is a plan that describes what information must be communicated to whom, by whom, when, and in what manner. It is a process of ensuring timely and appropriate collection, generation, storage, dissemination, and ultimate disposition of project information. This plan must be reviewed and updated regularly to ensure it continues to meet the communication needs.

Example: Communication Planning for Organizing a Conference

Mark has been assigned the responsibility of organizing a conference cosponsored by his company and a few other major companies in the industry. He has to communicate with different people at different levels of management across the various companies. The communication plan may include contact information of the key players in these companies and may stipulate email as the preferred mode of communication.

Information Distribution

Information distribution is the process of making information available to the project stakeholders in a timely manner. It does not only include implementation of the communication management plan, but also any unanticipated requests for information.

How to Create a Communication Plan

Effective communication management plans ensure that all project team members are aware of the type and format of information to be shared with project stakeholders.

Guidelines

To create an effective communication management plan, follow these guidelines:

- Determine a collection and filing structure that describes the methods the project team will use to collect and file project information.
- Determine the communication needs of project stakeholders. As a rule of thumb, project team members require more detail on a more frequent basis. Senior management typically requires summary information on a less frequent basis.
    - Work from an organization chart to avoid omitting a key stakeholder.
    - Ask for your project sponsor's input.
    - Ask open-ended questions.
- Analyze the value of providing the information to the project.
- Evaluate any constraints and assumptions to determine their possible impact on communication planning.
- Determine the appropriate communication technologies to use for communicating project information.
    - Determine the immediacy of the need for information.
    - Analyze the availability of technology systems.
    - Evaluate the expected project staff to identify their knowledge of and access to proposed technology.
    - Conduct research to determine the likelihood that there will be changes to the proposed technology before the project is over.
- Determine a distribution structure describing to whom and by whom project information, such as status reports, data schedules, meeting minutes, and so on, should be provided.
- Arrive at schedules for the production of each type of communication.
- Determine methods for accessing information between scheduled communications.
- Specify a method for updating and refining the communication management plan throughout the project life cycle.
- Integrate the communication management plan into the overall project plan.
- Distribute the plan to project stakeholders.

Example: Creating Communication Plan to Handle Issues

You are handling a project in which several tasks have been outsourced to another company. There are a lot of communication issues, with team members missing vital project information. You have decided to come up with a communication plan by consulting the stakeholders. You have made final that all documentation be placed on a shared location that all team members can access. Communication between the team members in your company and the employees of the external company should be by email. You also identified members of the external company who will receive status reports and the minutes of the meetings you conduct internally. Finally, you send the communication plan to the stakeholders for their approval.

ACTIVITY 4-2
Creating a Communication Management Plan

Scenario:
You have assembled your team. While most of your team is local, several key members are geographically dispersed across several states. You now need to define how your project team will communicate with each other.

What You Do	How You Do It

1. **Given the scenario, what would be a good primary communication technology for exchanging project information?**

    a) Email and phone exchange

    b) Weekly meetings

    c) Voice mail

    d) Video conferencing

2. **True or False? Keeping the stakeholders continuously informed about updates and status reports are indispensable for achieving your project objectives.**

    ___ True

    ___ False

3. **After integrating the communication management plan into the overall project plan, what would be the next logical step?**

    a) Creating a description of stakeholder communication requirements.

    b) Creating a schedule for the production of each type of communication.

    c) Distributing the plan to all the stakeholders.

    d) Determining whether there will be changes to the proposed technology before the project is over.

TOPIC C
Plan for Change Control

Now that you have planned the communication, you also need to plan for the changes in your project so that you can minimize any negative impact. In this topic, you will plan for change control.

Change is inevitable and unavoidable in any project. But, you need to make sure that none of the customers, stakeholders, or members of the project management team are surprised by delays to your scope and schedule, or by significant cost overruns. By developing a change control process for your project, documenting its parameters, and adhering to its guidelines, you can move ahead positively.

Need for Change Control

Change control is the process of identifying, documenting, approving or rejecting, and controlling changes to the project baselines. It reduces risks to your project by governing the execution of proposed changes that will affect scope, schedule, cost, and quality; it allows project managers to record the changes that are requested, make sure that changes are implemented in a standardized and approved manner, minimize their disruptive effect, and monitor their progression from initial request through completion.

> There may already be an approved change control process in your organization, in which case it is your responsibility to implement it for your project. If not, it is your responsibility to develop one for your project.

How to Plan for Change Control

By developing a change control plan, documenting its parameters, and adhering to its guidelines, you can reduce the risk to your project and maintain its momentum.

Guidelines

To develop a change control plan, follow these guidelines:

- Identify what will be considered a change that is significant enough to require management approval. For the sake of maintaining forward momentum on project work, project managers will not bring minor changes to schedule and cost estimates to the top management for approval.
- Gather any relevant historical data within the organization that relates to the process of identifying, documenting, approving or rejecting, and controlling changes to the project baselines.
- Determine the latitude the team would have in making autonomous decisions about changes.

- In conversation with stakeholders and the project management team, identify these responsible parties:
    - The people who are able to initiate change requests. These may include stakeholders, project management team members, and customers, among others.
    - The parties who are authorized to give or withhold business approval to a request for a change. Who will make the decision about whether or not a change is necessary and appropriate?
    - Who has the authority to approve additional funding, overtime costs, purchase orders, and so on?
    - The parties who will be responsible for executing the work necessary to satisfy the requested change, as well as evaluating the work for quality assurance.
    - The person(s) who will be responsible for managing changes. In some organizations, this may be the project manager, but in other organizations, it may be one or more functional managers.
    - The parties who are responsible for prioritizing changes and making qualitative decisions about them. Is this change imperative to the success of the project, or merely nice to have if time and resources allow?
- Identify how change requests must be approved. Some organizations might require written approval from customers before changes to the scope, schedule baseline, and budget can be implemented.
- Make sure that the organizational expectations regarding change control have been clearly defined and documented.

Example: Change Control Planning for the Conference Project

The project manager for the conference project identified that there are too many decision makers in the project which could be hazardous. Change of key speakers and topics of discussion could have a serious impact on the success of the project. He wants to carry out the changes of the project in a methodical manner and so, he decides to create a change control plan. He begins by gathering relevant information and documentation. He then proceeds to identify the key players within the team who can initiate change requests. He also identifies key stakeholders who will have the authority to approve the change requests. Finally, he documents all the information.

DISCOVERY ACTIVITY 4-3
Developing a Change Control Plan

Scenario:
The cookbook project has a very tight deadline, as well as a strict budget. You are concerned that any possible changes could negatively affect project performance baselines. You need to ensure that there is a standardized method for handling changes to the project work.

1. **Who will you involve in the change control planning for the cookbook project?**
    a) Francesca Tosca
    b) Key stakeholders
    c) Team members
    d) Implementation team members

2. **True or False? Only stakeholders are authorized to initiate a change request.**
    ___ True
    ___ False

3. **Who would make the decision about whether or not a change is necessary?**
    a) Stakeholders
    b) Stakeholders and the project team
    c) Core team members
    d) The project team

4. **True or False? Changes in a project do not usually affect the quality of the project.**
    ___ True
    ___ False

Lesson 4 Follow-up

In this lesson, you planned for project risks, communication, and change control. This will help you ensure that your project is conducted with the appropriate internal integrity and oversight.

1. **How would a project benefit from comprehensive risk planning?**

2. **Is the change control process in your organization effective? How? If not, how can it be improved?**

5 Managing a Project

Lesson Time: 1 hour(s), 15 minutes

Lesson Objectives:

In this lesson, you will manage a project.

You will:
- Begin project work.
- Execute project plan.
- Track project progress.
- Report performance.
- Implement change control.

Introduction

You finished your project planning and integrated the outputs from each of the planning processes into a comprehensive project management plan. Now you may want to transition your project from planning to execution. In this lesson, you will execute a project plan.

The project team members need a coach to guide them as they undertake the work defined in the scope statement. Executing a project plan ensures that your team is on the same page and that the project is completed on time, within budget, and with the required quality.

TOPIC A
Begin Project Work

Your project has officially advanced from the planning stage to execution. Now it's finally time to get started with project work. In this topic, you will begin project work.

All the planning for the project work is done. But, unless you get people to work, you may not be able to meet the project objectives. By bringing all of your team members together and giving them an insight into the goal of the project, you can successfully embark on your project.

The Team Acquisition Process

The team acquisition process involves identifying team members based on the skills matrix and computing associated costs based on the competencies of each of them. The project manager acquires the resources for the project. During acquisition, the project manager may have to negotiate with the functional manager for the appropriate resources needed for the project. Resources are often pooled within the organization, but they can also be acquired from outside sources with the help of the human resources team or consultants. Cost is the primary criteria when a team member is contracted from outside.

Kick-Off Meetings

A kick-off meeting is conducted by the project manager at the beginning of a project. The meeting is attended by the stakeholders of the project. It is designed to herald the opening of the project work, share information about its importance, articulate project scope, clarify individual as well as project objectives, generate excitement about the work at hand, and secure the enthusiastic participation of all the players. Kick-off meetings are generally held for all projects, but it is recommended for large projects, projects involving new processes or tools, or projects involving new contributors or newly formed teams.

How to Begin Project Work

By acquiring a project team and ensuring that all the team members understand the project goals and objectives, you can increase the probability of achieving the project's objectives.

Guidelines
To effectively begin the project work, follow these guidelines:

- Conduct a kick-off meeting.
- Call for one team member to take the responsibility of scribing important project specific information.
- Make sure that all team members and sponsors unanimously understand the project charter.
- Review the project plan with contributors.
- Define roles and responsibilities.
- Outline the resources that will be available to the team.
- Have the project sponsor explain why the project's work is important and how its goals are aligned with the larger organizational objectives.
- Document all the decisions and follow-up actions decided in the kick-off meeting.

- Discuss the organizational policies and procedures that the organization has in place regarding project execution to ensure predictable and consistent results. Make sure that all contractors are familiar with the procedures and comply with them.
- In line with good project management practice, use the artifacts necessary to get the job done. Use the organization's project management infrastructure. If it is not there already, then invent it.
- Be vigilant in collecting project information from stakeholders and sponsors.

Example:

The project on the preparation of a training manual is into the execution phase. Richard, the project manager, has invited all the stakeholders, sponsors, and the team members to a kick-off meeting. He requests someone in the team to take care of the minutes of the meeting, and Kate volunteers to do it. During the meeting, the team discusses the work to be done in the project and the responsibilities of each team member. The team decides to meet every Friday to review the work accomplished in the week and assess the progress of the project. If problems are identified, the team will analyze them and update the plan accordingly.

DISCOVERY ACTIVITY 5-1
Beginning Project Work

Scenario:
You have been asked to serve as the project manager for a short-term initiative coming up within your department. You need to design a questionnaire and distribute it to a large number of employees and then tabulate the results. The questionnaire is meant to determine the employees' opinions on a number of significant issues. You will be working with a small team of contributors.

1. You need to decide whether to host a kick-off meeting. Which should be one of your considerations?

    a) To generate enthusiasm about the work at hand.

    b) To educate the customer about your work processes.

    c) To know external customer's expectations.

    d) To know the budget of this project.

2. If you decide to hold a kick-off meeting, whom should you include?

    a) HR team

    b) Sponsors

    c) All the contributors

    d) All the employees

3. True or False? The project manager need not necessarily define the roles and responsibilities of all the team members.

    __ True

    __ False

TOPIC B
Execute the Project Plan

You have acquired your project team and have conducted a project kick-off meeting. It is now finally time to start leveraging the plan. In this topic, you will execute the project plan.

Coordinating people and other resources to carry out the project plan is like conducting an orchestra. Effectively directing and managing project execution ensures that the project team starts and finishes the project work according to the project management plan.

The Project Execution Process

The project execution process involves carrying out the project plan to produce a product or provide a service. It requires the project team to build on the foundation laid during project plan development. The project manager coordinates, directs, and monitors the progress of the project. This is not just one coherent task, but is a lengthy and complex iterative process.

Quality Assurance

Quality Assurance (QA) is a method of evaluating overall project performance through planned, systematic activities; it creates confidence that the project will adhere to the appropriate processes and satisfy standards for quality. It is a part of a continuum of quality activities that begin in the initiating and planning processes and continue throughout the project. It is iterative and it may be adapted based on the identification and resolution of quality problems over the project's life cycle. The quality assurance process varies with the needs of each project.

How to Execute the Project Plan

Throughout the entire execution of a project, the project manager can employ various techniques to coordinate and direct the various technical and organizational aspects of the project. Implementing these techniques throughout the project execution will ensure the success of the project.

Guidelines

To effectively execute the project plan, follow these guidelines:

- Ensure that the project starts and finishes on time, within the budget, and within scope.

- Comply with any organizational policies and procedures that the organization has in place regarding project execution to ensure predictable and consistent results. Make sure that all contractors are familiar with and comply with the procedures.

- Decide on a system that will allow you to formally sanction work to commence on an activity or deliverable. The value of the control that your system provides should be balanced with the cost (money and time) of designing, implementing, and using the system.

- Praise and motivate the contributors.
  - Advertise their success. Send out congratulatory email announcements to the whole group when individual contributors make their deadlines or meet the project's requirements.
  - Thank contributors for their efforts, both on an individual basis and publicly, during meetings. Note that if you are singling people out for praise, make sure you include everyone who has contributed to avoid inadvertently hurting anyone's feelings.
- Plan and conduct regularly scheduled status review meetings to exchange information concerning the status of work, change requests, and preventive and corrective action:
  - Before the meeting, send a list of open tasks to all participants, so that they can prepare to discuss task status.
  - During the meeting, address each task on the task list by asking the person responsible for the task to report on whether the task has begun, if it has been completed, and how much labor had been spent on it.
  - If problems are identified during a status review meeting, assign them as actions to a responsible person, making sure to include a deadline for resolution. List them on the issues log to be reviewed at a later meeting.
  - Review all outstanding issues. Work through the issues log to check the progress of all the issues listed as outstanding from previous meetings. If necessary, assign additional resources.
  - To encourage participation and commitment, avoid making project status meetings into group disciplinary proceedings. If you feel that an individual team member is not performing adequately, schedule a private meeting with the person to review the matter later.

Example:

The project plan for the research project is ready and the project team has begun the work on time. You circulated emails on the organization's policies and procedures and the compliance requirements of the client that the project team needs to adhere to. You decide to meet with the team twice a week to discuss the status of the project and review outstanding issues, if any.

DISCOVERY ACTIVITY 5-2
Executing the Project Plan

Scenario:
Your team has gathered for a regular project meeting. Everyone is surprised to find a cake and a cooler with sodas in the room. You announce that this meeting celebrates the official transition of the project from planning to execution. After everyone has had a chance to sample the cake, you settle down to business and review the company memorandum on work authorization.

1. True or False? The team can go ahead with project work after Annie Hodgson, the project sponsor, offers verbal authorization to commence work.

    ___ True

    ___ False

2. When you begin project execution, what should you do?

    a) Ensure that the funding has been approved.

    b) Comply with organizational policies and procedures.

    c) Conduct status meeting.

    d) Learn who the stakeholders are.

3. True or False? Conducting weekly team meetings helps in ensuring that the project schedule completion dates are met.

    ___ True

    ___ False

4. Your team needs to design a questionnaire, which is one of the primary tasks in the project. What should you do to help them?

    a) Make sure they finish it on time.

    b) Make sure that the questionnaire is attractive.

    c) Monitor their general work performance and keep an eye on how well they adhere to company policies.

    d) Make sure they design it the way you would do it.

TOPIC C
Track Project Progress

You project is now well into execution. You now need to track the performance of the project progress so that you can be sure that your project is heading in the right direction. In this topic, you will track project performance.

You want to be able to monitor the progress of your project from its initial kick-off through completion, so that you can ensure that your project will be delivered on time, on specification, and within the budget. By tracking the contributors' progress against the schedule, identifying common performance problems and red flags that may indicate problems, and negotiating solutions as necessary, you will be able to bring about a successful result.

Earned Value Analysis

Earned value analysis is a method of measuring the performance of a project. It analyzes the project progress by comparing actual schedule and cost performance against planned performance as laid out in the cost and schedule baselines. By this method, you can identify whether the project is on time and within the budget.

Earned Value Calculations

Earned value calculations help you determine if a project work is happening as per the plan. There are several terms involved in earned value calculations.

Term	Description
Budget At Completion (BAC)	It is the total sum of the budget for a project.
Planned Value (PV)	It is the budgeted cost to be spent on a task within a period of time.
Actual Cost (AC)	It is the total cost incurred in accomplishing a task within a period of time.
Earned Value (EV)	It is the value of work actually accomplished. It is calculated by multiplying the percentage of work completed by the Budget At Completion (BAC).

Variance Identification

Variance identification is the process of measuring the differences between the actual project performance and the planned performance. The most commonly used variance measures are cost variance and schedule variance.

Variance Measure	Description
Schedule Variance (SV)	The difference between the work actually performed and the work scheduled. The formula to find out the schedule variance is SV=EV-PV. A positive variance indicates that your project is ahead of plan and a negative variance indicates that it is progressing behind schedule.
Cost Variance (CV)	It is the difference between the planned cost of work performed and the actual cost incurred. This will help us to find out whether the project is exceeding or falling within its estimated cost. Cost variance can be calculated by using this formula CV=EV-AC. A positive variance indicates that your project is under spending and a negative variance indicates that it is over spending.

Performance Indices

Performance indices are used to measure the progress of project toward the set goals.

Performance Index	Description
Cost Performance Index (CPI)	Cost Performance Index (CPI) is a measurement of cost performance that can be used to determine whether the project is over or under budget. To calculate CPI, you need to divide the earned value (EV) by the actual cost (AC).
Schedule Performance Index (SPI)	Schedule Performance Index (SPI) is the ratio of work performed to work scheduled. To calculate the SPI, you need to divide the EV by the PV.

Variance Management

Variance management is a method of measuring the variances and taking corrective actions in order to achieve the planned outcome. The first step in variance management is performing a root cause analysis at each task level to find out what led to the fall. Once it is identified, the root problem should be worked upon based on real world knowledge and its effect on the project as a whole. When the ideal work around is identified, you need to present the information to the stakeholders to decide if it can be applied.

Forecasting Techniques

Forecasting techniques are used to determine the expected costs needed to complete a project work or an activity in entirety.

Forecasting Technique	Description
Estimate To Complete (ETC)	Helps to find how much more it is going to cost to complete the project. It can be calculated by using these formulas: ● ETC=(BAC-EV) – This formula is used when the current variance is not expected to continue in future. ● ETC=(BAC-EV)/CPI – This can be used when the current variances are seen as typical of future variances.
Estimate At Complete (EAC)	Represents the projected final costs of work when completed. It can be calculated using this formula: EAC= ETC+AC.
Variance At Completion (VAC)	Is the difference between estimate at completion (EAC) and budget at completion (BAC).

How to Track Project Progress

Effectively tracking project progress ensures successful project outcome.

Guidelines

To effectively track project progress, follow these guidelines:

- Analyze work results against planned performance based on performance elements defined during the planning processes.
  - Involve the team members who are closest to the work in the data analysis. They are the people who understand the work and can probably identify appropriate corrective actions for resolving variances.
  - Use Earned Value techniques to assess cost and schedule progress against planned performance.
  - Evaluate the results of corrective actions to determine whether they have produced the desired results.
- Analyze the results of performance measurements by asking these questions:
  - Is there a variance?
  - What is the cause of the variance?
  - What is the magnitude of the variance? Is the activity causing the variance on the critical path?
  - Is it likely that the variance can be made up in the near future without corrective action or is corrective action necessary to bring the schedule performance back in line with the baseline?
- Hold performance reviews to communicate and assess project status and progress.
- Identify and document corrective action to take, to bring expected future project performance in line with planned performance. Depending on the priorities of your project, consider one or more of the following alternatives:
  - Fast-tracking - Perform project activities which have originally been scheduled sequentially and concurrently.
  - Crashing - Allocate more resources to activities so that the project can be completed in less time.
  - Outsourcing - Secure services and expertise from an outside source on a contract or short-term basis.
  - Resource leveling - Readjust the work as appropriate so that people are not overly allocated.
  - Reducing project scope.
- Measure and monitor performance the same way throughout the project life cycle so that meaningful comparisons can be made.
- Document lessons learned during schedule control for use in future projects. The documentation should include:
  - Causes of variances.
  - Performance baselines affected by the changes and rationale behind the recommended corrective action.
  - Any other lessons learned during schedule control.

Example:

The research project is well into execution. But now, the project manager receives information from the team lead that an employee has gone on unplanned leave. He calls for a team meeting to assess the situation and take stock of the status of the project. By referring to the team skills matrix, he determines the role of the person on leave, identifies an alternative resource, and assigns that person to take up the work. The project manager also documents the problem, the corrective action taken, and the results of the corrective action.

DISCOVERY ACTIVITY 5-3
Calculating Earned Value

Scenario:
Your team has presented you with the following status data for the "Develop Recipes" work package:
- Planned Value (PV) = $7,500
- Earned Value (EV) = 40%
- Actual Cost (AC) = $2,500
- Number of days scheduled = 30
- Actual number of days = 20

1. **What is the earned value for this work package?**
    a) $7,500
    b) $5,000
    c) $3,000
    d) $2,500

2. **Calculate planned value for the "Develop Recipes" work package for the actual number of days.**
    a) $2,500
    b) $500
    c) $4,500
    d) $5,000

3. **What is the cost variance for the work package?**
    a) $3,000
    b) $2,500
    c) $1,000
    d) $500

4. **What does the cost variance indicate?**
    a) The project is over budget by $500.
    b) The project is under budget by $500.
    c) The project is over budget by $2,500.
    d) The project is under budget by $2,500.

5. **What formula would you use to calculate SPI?**

    a) EV-PV

    b) EV/PV

    c) EV-AC

    d) EV/AC

6. **Calculate the CPI for the project.**

    a) 1.4

    b) 0.1

    c) 1.2

    d) 0.2

7. **What does the Cost Performance Index (CPI) of 1.2 for the project indicate?**

    a) The project is performing under budget.

    b) The project is performing over budget.

    c) The project is within budget.

    d) The project is behind schedule and is over budget.

8. **True or False? SPI of 1.0 means the project is right on schedule.**

    __ True

    __ False

9. **Identify a benefit of conducting the earned value analysis.**

    a) It provides a more accurate project baseline than other tracking methods.

    b) It allows you to track project performance and also acts as a means to forecast project performance.

    c) Management can understand earned value analysis better than other measures.

    d) Helps identify what the project team has accomplished so far.

10. **Your team has been working in tandem ever since the project started. But, over the past couple of weeks you have observed a dip in performance. What steps can you take to help the team perform better?**

    a) During team meetings, shower praise on members who performed well and condemn the nonperformers.

    b) Tighten the deadlines to improve productivity.

    c) Encourage team members to share their experiences with others.

    d) Appreciate good efforts during team meetings and organize events for recognizing team members who have performed well.

TOPIC D
Report Performance

You have tracked the progress of a project. Now you would like to keep the stakeholders informed about the current status of the project. In this topic, you will report project performance.

As a project manager, you need to communicate project performance to the top management, stakeholders, and customers, and reassure them that the work is on time and within budget. Effective performance reporting enables you—as well as your team members, sponsors, stakeholders, and customers—to make reasoned, informed, and timely decisions regarding projects.

Performance Reporting

Performance reporting is the process of gathering and communicating information regarding the current status of a project as well as projections for progress over time. During performance reporting, information regarding the work being accomplished and resources being used is collected, analyzed, and displayed in various report formats. The performance reports help to compare the current execution status of the project with the originally approved plans and identify deviations. They also serve as historical information that may be used in future projects.

Types of Performance Reports

There are three types of performance reports, status reports, progress reports, and forecast reports.

Report Type	Description
Status report	Describes what has been achieved in the current period, what is the current status of the budget, scope, and schedules, what issues, risks, and variances have been identified and how to correct them, and what has been planned for the next period.
Progress report	Gives a summary of the progress of the project towards its objectives, provides historical progress information of the project from its initiation, and compares the progress made so far to the progress that was originally expected.
Forecast report	Projects the timelines and cost of a project for a future period based on the current status of the project.

Personnel Evaluations

Personnel evaluations involve tracking the performance of team members and providing feedback. The project manager needs to perform formal or informal assessments of team members throughout a project's life cycle to manage conflicts, resolve issues, and appraise the performance of individual team members. Personnel evaluations help managers to identify whether the team members require training and to organize training on technical or soft skills as required. It also enables him to plan for recognition events to motivate the team, and improve the team's competencies and sentiments to help them perform better.

How to Report Performance

Communicating information using performance reports helps the team pinpoint problems that may need to be resolved. It also enhances the team's ability to implement corrective actions early enough to make a positive difference to the end result of a project.

Guidelines

To effectively report project performance, follow these guidelines:

- Consult your project plan's subsidiary plans for guidelines and procedures for reporting on the various aspects of project performance.
- Determine the type of report needed for the information being reported. Make sure that the format of the report adequately provides the type of information and level of detail required by various stakeholders.
- Prepare performance reports that provide the required information in a format that enhances understanding of the material. Formal reports should contain:
  - A cover page with the project name, project manager's name, type of report, and date of report.
  - A description of the project's actual accomplishments for the reporting period as compared to the goals established for the period. In addition, any changes implemented or anticipated should be described.
  - Interim performance reports should include a forecast of how the project is expected to perform in the future.
  - End of project reports should include a brief description of major accomplishments, an evaluation of the project's performance, an explanation of any variances in the performance and project objectives, and any future plans for the project.
  - Appendices, which may include any supporting material that contributes to an understanding of the project and its progress to date, such as charts, tables, and samples.
- Balance the cost, time, and logistics of preparing performance reports against the benefits gained by the reporting.

Example:

The project manager of a construction project has to present reports on the project's performance to the stakeholders. He consolidates the information on variances from the agreed baselines as per the guidelines and procedures laid down in the project plan.

The project manager creates a status report detailing the accomplishments in the current reporting period, highlighting the current status of the costs, scope, and schedules. The team had to deal with unexpected increases in steel prices in the current period. The project manager presents this as the reason behind the huge cost variances.

Though there has been a sharp increase in costs, the project team has identified areas where cost reduction methods can be applied. The project manager will present this information to the stakeholders while explaining how the project will progress further.

DISCOVERY ACTIVITY 5-4
Reporting Project Performance

Scenario:
As the project manager of the Italian cookbook project, you have to inform the stakeholders about the current status of the project and explain whether the project will meet its objectives. Though you have calculated variances, it is important to present them in a format that will help the stakeholders figure out how the project is progressing and foresee its position in the future.

1. **What information does a status report convey to the stakeholders?**

    a) The exemplary performance of one of the assistant chefs.

    b) A prediction of the final cost the project will incur.

    c) A description of the project costs and schedules for the current reporting period.

    d) The conflicts between the team members and how the project manager resolved them.

2. **What is a benefit of a project forecast report to the project team and the senior management?**

    a) Pinpoints the problem areas of the project.

    b) Identifies where the project will stand if it progresses at the current rate.

    c) Identifies the team members responsible for the projected success or failure of the project.

    d) Analyzes the status of the project as against original plans.

3. **True or False? Personnel evaluations help to identify the training requirements of a project team.**

    __ True

    __ False

TOPIC E
Implement Change Control

Now that you have executed the project plan and have taken steps to make sure that your project is conducted with appropriate integrity and oversight, you will go further by controlling the changes to the project work, budget, and schedule baseline. In this topic, you will implement the change control plan.

Sometimes you may have to make sure that none of the customers, stakeholders, or members of the project management team are surprised by sudden change in scope, delays to your schedule or significant cost overruns. By controlling the changes in your project, documenting its parameters, and adhering to the change control guidelines, you can reduce the risk to your project and maintain its positive forward movement.

Elements of a Change Request

Change Requests are formal documents, letters, memos, or even meeting minutes, that describe a request for change and the implications of the change to the project. It contains certain basic elements of information in it.

Element	Description
Change	Describe the change requested. Include specific criteria that can be used to measure the change.
Requested By	Who is requesting the change.
Reason for Change	Why the change is being made; how the change will benefit the outcome of the project.
Method of Change	How the change will be implemented.
Affected Parties	Who will be affected by the change.
Affect on Success Criteria	How will the change affect: • Scope • Time • Cost • Quality
Backup Information	Any additional information that is needed to support or explain the nature of the change.
Sign-offs	Who approved the change.
Date of Approval	When was the change approved.

How to Implement Change Control

Procedure Reference: Implement Change Control

To implement change control:

1. When a change request has been submitted, justify why it should be investigated.
2. Analyze the change request.
3. Document and communicate the change request.
4. Determine the impact of change on the project.
5. If necessary, get back to the requester with questions.
6. Discuss the change and its impact with the stakeholders.
7. Get sign-off from all stakeholders on actions to be taken.
8. Update the project plan to include the changes made and then proceed with the your allocated task.

DISCOVERY ACTIVITY 5-5
Implementing Change Control

Scenario:
You are working on a PM Training Roll-out project that has a very tight deadline as well as a strict budget. You are concerned that some requested changes could negatively affect project performance baselines. You need to ensure that the changes do not affect project work, budget, and schedule baseline.

1. **The IT department informs you that the project software upgrade will have a significant delay in delivery. The software includes many new enhancements that will replace the current project management information system reporting process and should be included in the training. In the risk management plan, you accounted for a delay due to the software upgrade, but this delay is much longer than originally anticipated. What action should you take?**

    a) Bring information to all the team members for evaluation.

    b) Coordinate changes across knowledge areas.

    c) Identify corrective action to be taken to resolve the problem.

    d) Bring information to all the key stakeholders.

    e) Update the project plan to reflect changes.

2. **Who will you involve in the change control process for the PM Training Roll-out project?**

    a) People involved in the PM Training Roll-out project.

    b) All the team members.

    c) Key stakeholders.

    d) Implementation team members.

3. **True or False? Change requests should be justified before analysis.**

    ___ True

    ___ False

Lesson 5 Follow-up

In this lesson, you managed project execution. Executing a job according to the project plan ensures that your team is on the same page and that your project finishes on time, within budget, and with the required quality.

1. **In your experience, what aspects of executing the project plan have you found to be the most challenging? Why?**

2. **What techniques would you use to execute future projects effectively?**

6 | Executing the Project Closeout Phase

Lesson Time: 25 minutes

Lesson Objectives:

In this lesson, you will execute the project closeout phase.

You will:
- Close a project.
- Create a final report.

Introduction

You have successfully executed the project plan and obtained all deliverables from the project team. You are ready to hand over the project to the customer. In this lesson, you will execute the project closeout phase.

Unfinished business, contracts not correctly closed out, and poor documentation can turn into months of additional work and expenditures. The last thing you do on a project will be the first thing people remember about your efforts overall. Formal project closure helps ensure that there are no loose ends that could unravel the good work of your team and the success of your project.

TOPIC A
Close a Project

You implemented the project plan and executed all project activities. It is time now to bring the project to a formal conclusion and handover the deliverables to the stakeholders. In this topic, you will close out a project.

Ending a project requires the same care and attention as starting a project. It is necessary to ensure that stakeholders are satisfied with the project's outcome. Obtaining the stakeholders' formal acceptance of your project's outcome ensures that the project is properly closed.

Closeout Elements

Project closeout involves many elements that are documented and archived.

Element	Description
Project Outcome	The final product, service, or result that the project was expected to produce.
Project Files	A collection of all the documents produced during the course of the project.
Formal Acceptance Documentation	Documentation that confirms that the stakeholders have formally accepted that the project has met the requirements and that the deliverables satisfy the specifications.
Project Closure Documents	Formal documentation indicating project completion. If the project got terminated before completion, this documentation specifies the reasons for the termination.
Historical Information	Lesson learned and other information to be archived for future reference.
Contract Documentation	Documents containing the contract information of the resources.
Reports	Project performance reports, performance evaluation reports, and any other reports generated throughout the project.

The Project Closeout Process

The *project closeout* process involves closing out all activities and formally ending the project or, in the case of multiphase projects, closing out a specific project phase. It coordinates activities needed to verify and document project deliverables, to obtain the stakeholders' acceptance of the deliverables, to confirm that the project has met all requirements, and to identify reasons if a project is terminated before completion. Upon completion of these activities, the process authorizes a formal handoff of project deliverables to the stakeholders. The process also includes other activities to collect project records, analyze project success or failure, archive project information and lessons learned, release resources, and close contracts.

How to Close a Project

Procedure Reference: Close a Project

To close a project:

1. Prepare a project termination checklist that may be useful when closing out a project or phase. This helps to ensure that you are thorough in your closeout.
2. Gather and organize performance measurement documentation, product documentation, and other relevant project records for easy review by stakeholders.
3. Release project resources.
4. Update records to ensure that they reflect final specifications. Be sure to update the resource pool database to reflect new skills and increased levels of proficiency.
5. Analyze project success and effectiveness and document lessons learned.
6. Prepare lessons learned reports and a final project report.
7. Obtain project approval. Demonstrate to the customer or sponsor that the deliverables meet the defined acceptance criteria to obtain formal acceptance of the phase or project. This may involve preparing an end-of-project report or giving a presentation.
8. Archive a complete set of indexed project records.
9. Celebrate the success of the project with the team and other stakeholders.

DISCOVERY ACTIVITY 6-1
Closing a Project

Scenario:
Your good planning and control has resulted in the Italian cookbook project coming to a successful close. The final project deliverable is complete. It is now time to hand over the project to the stakeholders and bring it to a formal conclusion.

1. **What is an element of project closeout that requires the stakeholders' acceptance?**

    a) Recipes not included in the cookbook.

    b) Minutes of all project status meetings.

    c) The final draft of the cookbook.

    d) Documentation of lessons learned from the project.

2. **What project information is important and needs to be archived for future reference?**

    a) Recipe testing activities and photo shooting activities for the illustrations.

    b) The deviations in the project schedules, reasons for the deviations, and steps taken to keep the project on track.

    c) Francesca Tosca's autograph and photographs with the project team.

    d) Variances between planned cost and actual cost, and steps taken to keep the project as much within budget as possible.

3. **True or False? You need to bring Francesca Tosca's contract agreement to a formal closure as part of the project closeout process.**

    ___ True

    ___ False

4. **What activity will you perform as part of the project closeout process?**

    a) Collect anecdotes from Francesca Tosca.

    b) Obtain a formal acceptance of the project deliverables from the stakeholders.

    c) Shoot pictures of the food cooked while recipe testing.

    d) Bring major project issues to the notice of the senior management.

TOPIC B
Create a Final Report

You have performed the project closeout operations. Now, you may need to summarize all that happened in the project and make information available to the management. In this topic, you will create a final report.

The successful completion of a project does not imply that everything went on smoothly throughout the project's life cycle. There might have been problems with resources, schedule conflicts, or any other issue that the project manager and his team have encountered and tackled successfully. Documenting these information as a final report and presenting it to the stakeholders and the senior management will not only bring out the efforts put in or the decisions taken by the project team, but would also help the management to take informed decisions while handling similar projects in the future.

Final Report

The *final report* is a report that summarizes what happened in the project. It is prepared for all projects, irrespective of whether a project has been completed successfully or not. It presents an overview of the project, an evaluation of the team's performance, a list of issues encountered, a summary of what went right and what wrong, a commentary on the deviations from the original plan and budget, a summary of major accomplishments of the project team, and a record of recommendations for future projects. The final report is made available to the senior management, stakeholders, and other project managers to apply the experience in future projects.

How to Create a Final Report

The final report documents all that happened in a project for future reference.

Guidelines

To create an effective final report, follow these guidelines:

- Make a summary of how the project was carried out.
  - Provide an overview of the project's initial objectives and specifications.
  - Explain any changes to objectives and specifications, the reasons behind the changes, and how the changes were executed.
  - Present the original project plans, list revisions to those plans if any, and provide reasons for the revisions.
  - Present the initial budget, identify the actual project costs, and explain variances if any.
  - Describe the deliverables of each phase.
  - If the project was terminated prior to completion, state reasons for the same.

- Evaluate the performance of the project team.
  - Comment on the performance of each individual on the project team.
  - Highlight the major accomplishments of the project team.
  - Comment on the relationship between the project team, the stakeholders, and the senior management.
  - Acknowledge the contributions of the project team.
  - Identify mistakes committed and bring poor performance to notice.
  - Explain any conflicts in the team and how they were resolved.
- Explain the issues encountered.
  - Identify the issues encountered throughout the project's life cycle and explain how they were tackled.
  - List any issues that could not be resolved.
- Provide recommendations for future projects of a similar kind.
  - Explain lessons learned in the project and provide suggestions for better performance.
  - Suggest changes in the existing policies and procedures.
  - Bring out new ideas for improving project performance.

Example:

You are the manager for a project to create a website for your company. Now that you have completed the project, you are preparing the final report. In the final report, you start by providing an overview of the project's initial objectives and specifications, highlighting key changes to the objectives, and explaining how the changes were carried out. You are also providing comparisons between the planned dates and the actual dates in which deliverables were completed. As part of the evaluation of the project team's performance, you are highlighting the major accomplishments of the team. After describing all that happened in this project, you also provide recommendations for projects of similar kind.

DISCOVERY ACTIVITY 6-2
Creating a Final Report

Scenario:
The stakeholders of the Italian cookbook project have approved the project's deliverables and you have performed all the activities pertaining to the formal conclusion of the project. Though the project has been completed successfully, you encountered many issues during its life cycle. You would like to document all such information so that it is helpful for project managers handling similar projects in future.

1. **What information would you include in the final report of the Italian cookbook project?**
   a) A list of files and documentation generated during the project's life cycle.
   b) Documentation of the contract signed with Francesca Tosca.
   c) The outstanding coordination within the project team that ensured completion of the project on time and within budget.
   d) One of the assistant chefs met with an accident and the rest of the assistant chefs had to share the extra work among themselves.

2. **True or False? The final report is presented to the stakeholders, the project team, and the senior management.**
   ___ True
   ___ False

3. **One of the assistant chefs was a wonderful worker. She always showed up prepared, worked hard and smart, and was willing to do more than her share of project tasks. However, she skipped or was late for at least 50 percent of the team meetings. What commentary would you include while evaluating her performance in the final report?**
   a) The assistant chef's unwillingness to participate in team meetings made things more difficult for others on the team.
   b) She made group decision making harder.
   c) She made team communication more complex, and her absence was probably a morale buster.
   d) Though she was unwilling to attend the meetings, her work compensated her behavior.

4. **What is a valid recommendation for future projects?**

   a) Hire Francesca Tosca as the chef for all future cookbook projects as she demands less compensation.

   b) Strive to complete projects before scheduled time by stretching the working time of resources.

   c) Establish a communication protocol among the project team and stakeholders.

   d) Compensate on the quality of the product if the cost to the company can be reduced.

Lesson 6 Follow-up

In this lesson, you executed the closeout phase of a project. This enables you to formally hand off the project and deliverables to the stakeholders, and bring the project to a completion.

1. **What lessons have you learned from your project? What major issues arose and how were they resolved?**

2. **What are the major accomplishments of your project team? How would you highlight this information in the final report?**

Follow-up

In this course, you examined the elements of sound project management and applied its generally recognized practices to manage projects. You now have the skills and knowledge required to successfully manage projects in your organization.

1. **How do you think applying project management practices will help you manage projects successfully?**

2. **What project management processes does your organization follow? Are there any formal processes that are not carried out?**

What's Next?

To expand your knowledge in project management, you may take the *Certified Associate in Project Management (CAPM®)* course.

Lesson Labs

Due to classroom setup constraints, some labs cannot be keyed in sequence immediately following their associated lesson. Your instructor will tell you whether your labs can be practiced immediately following the lesson or whether they require separate setup from the main lesson content.

Project Management Fundamentals: (Second Edition)

Lesson 1 Lab 1
Reviewing the Key Elements of Project Management

Activity Time: 10 minutes

Scenario:
You have been assigned to manage the project on designing a web page for the Our Global Company website. You would like to review your knowledge of the key elements of project management before you start managing the project.

1. Which term is used to refer to work that is ongoing and produces the same outcome every time it is carried out?

    a) Program

    b) Portfolio

    c) Project

    d) Operational task

2. Which stakeholder provides the financial assistance during a project's life cycle?

    a) Customer

    b) Project manager

    c) Sponsor

    d) Project management team

3. Which project management process defines a project and authorizes its start?

    a) Planning

    b) Execution

    c) Initiation

    d) Monitoring and Controlling

4. In which organizational structure are employees grouped based on their area of expertise?

    a) Projectized

    b) Functional

    c) Matrix

    d) Composite

5. **Which is a function of the PMO?**

    a) Approve project deliverables at every stage of a project.

    b) Supervise and coordinate management of all projects.

    c) Provide the funds required to complete a project.

    d) Provide resources required to complete a project.

Lesson 2 Lab 1
Initiating a Project

Activity Time: 15 minutes

Setup:
Listen to the direction provided by your instructor and participate in the group discussion.

Scenario:
The senior management of OGC has decided to implement a file sharing system for internal use. The system will enable OGC's employees to upload files and will serve as a repository to store information. The new system has been proposed as a replacement to the existing manual system. Rita, a member of the senior management team, is responsible for this project. She has assigned Betty as the project manager for this project. John is an experienced contributor who can help Betty in understanding the technical aspects of this project and Richard is a functional manager who can provide her historical information about similar past projects.

1. **Betty is clueless about the requirements of the project. What step does Betty need to take to get the requirements clarified? As it is a small project for the company's internal use, can she just assume the requirements or is there any other way she can get a better idea of the requirements?**

2. **Is it necessary for the scope statement to identify what features the new system will not support? Is it important for Betty to document this? If so, what can she do to come to a conclusion about what features the new system will provide and what it will not?**

3. Apart from the scope, what other constraining factors does Betty need to take into account? Do you think a clear understanding of project constraints is essential to complete a project successfully? Why?

4. Once the scope statement is ready, can Betty develop the project plan? Does she need to obtain the stakeholder's approval before starting work on the plan? How important is this approval going to be?

5. How will Betty know what resources she requires for this project? Is there any way she can help the management identify the skills required to complete the project work?

Lesson 3 Lab 1

Planning for Time

Activity Time: 10 minutes

Setup:

Listen to the direction provided by your instructor and participate in the group discussion.

Scenario:

Betty has prepared the scope statement and obtained the management's approval for the same. The scope statement provides the objectives of the project, its requirements, constraints, and assumptions. Betty has also identified the skills required for the project and presented the list of required resources to Rita.

Betty is looking forward to creating a project plan for the project team. Rita has suggested that Betty can seek the help of John and Annie who are experienced contributors. They can help her identify the individual project activities and estimate the durations required to complete them.

1. The scope statement does identify the project deliverables. But, what is the best possible way to organize the project work?

2. How would Betty know that the level of decomposition in the WBS is sufficient?

    Do you think John and Annie can help her in identifying the lowest possible amount of work?

3. How can Betty identify the activities in the project that cannot be delayed?

4. What aspects does Betty need to take into account while developing cost estimates?

Lesson 4 Lab 1
Planning for Communication and Change Control

Activity Time: 15 minutes

Setup:
Listen to the direction provided by your instructor and participate in the group discussion.

Scenario:
You are currently managing a project on creating a digital media drive for a multinational company. Some of your team members operate from different parts of the world. You are apprehensive about the method of communication to be used with the team members as they are located across borders. You would also have to manage the changes in the project, so that it does not affect the project adversely.

1. What would be the communication needs of your project team?

2. What are the challenges involved in creating the communications plan for your team? What are the facts you would take into consideration when creating the plan?

3. Which communication technology can be used to communicate important information effectively, while ensuring that it is not lost or misinterpreted? Why?

4. You have determined that there isn't a change control process in your organization. What problems could result in this situation? How do you plan to handle it?

5. What are the facts you would consider when creating the change control plan? What changes would you plan for in the given scenario?

Lesson 5 Lab 1
Managing a Book Project

Activity Time: 15 minutes

Setup:
Listen to the direction provided by your instructor and participate in the group discussion.

Scenario:
You have been asked by your manager, Rita Mascarenhas, to manage a book project for the upcoming anniversary celebration. Rita wants the project completed within the next four months, in time for the shareholders' conference. She has assigned several people on staff to work on this project. But this work wouldn't necessarily be anyone's first priority.

1. How would you indicate the start of the project to the team members? Who are the others whom you would keep informed about the fact that the project has started?

2. If a team members' availability for the project is a problem, how would you handle it?

3. In the given scenario, would it be possible to track the project progress at all? If yes, how would you be tracking the progress of the project? How will you handle variances, if any?

4. Your project work is almost complete, but you just got a notification from the team that there may be a delay of 24 hours in shipping the content for printing. Though it is a small delay considering the amount of work that the team has put in, will it affect your project in any way? Would you discuss this with your manager?

Lesson 6 Lab 1
Executing the Project Closeout Phase

Activity Time: 10 minutes

Scenario:
The project you are managing currently is approaching its conclusion. Before handing off the deliverables to the stakeholders, you would like to review the activities involved in closing a project formally.

1. What elements need to be documented and archived during the closeout process?
    a) Documents that confirm the stakeholders' acceptance of the deliverables.
    b) Details of phone conversations and meetings conducted with the team.
    c) A collection of all documents prepared during the project's life cycle.
    d) The initial calculations performed by the project manager to arrive at an estimate of the duration of project activities.

2. **Which is correct about a formal project handoff?**
    a) It is a good idea because it covers up all the mistakes of the project team.
    b) It can positively shape perceptions of the product by highlighting product benefits.
    c) It should only be held if the customer pays extra for this service.
    d) It should not be conducted if the project is terminated before completion.

3. **What information should a final report contain?**
    a) A summary of what went right and what went wrong in the project.
    b) A commentary on the deviations from the original plans and budget.
    c) A record of recommendations for future projects.
    d) A list of documents prepared throughout the project's life cycle.

4. **True or False? Documenting lessons learned and archiving project information will serve as a reference for project managers in the future.**
    ___ True
    ___ False

Solutions

Lesson 1

Activity 1-1

1. **Which is a characteristic of the project Rita's team is working on?**
   a) Performs the day-to-day activities of a business.
   b) Produces the same output every time.
   ✓ c) Has a definite beginning and a definite end.
   d) Is ongoing and repetitive.

2. **Match each stakeholder with the appropriate responsibility.**

   _c_ Project manager   a. An individual or group that provides financial resources for a project.

   _b_ Customer   b. An individual or organization that will use the project's output.

   _a_ Sponsor   c. An individual responsible for managing a project.

   _e_ Project team   d. The members of the project team who perform project management activities.

   _d_ Project management team   e. A group that performs the work in a project.

3. **True or False? Your team of tax return processors is assigned an operational task.**
   ✓ True
   __ False

4. **True or False? Rita's team performs a set of repetitive tasks and there is no outcome. Therefore, they are assigned an ongoing work activity.**
   __ True
   ✓ False

5. True or False? Managing Rita's project may be more difficult than managing your group of tax return processors because this project work has never been undertaken before, the team is multidisciplined with conflicting priorities, and the team also reports to other managers.

   ✓ True
   __ False

Activity 1-2

1. Which definition best describes project management?

   a) Management of a collection of programs to ensure that all projects in the collection contribute to achieving the organization's strategic goals.

   ✓ b) Management of project activities to meet project objectives through the application of knowledge, skills, tools, and techniques to those activities.

   c) Management of a collection of projects in a centralized and coordinated manner to achieve collective objectives and benefits.

   d) Management of day-to-day activities to sustain the business.

2. Match each term with its definition.

_b_	Project	a.	Collection of related projects that may have a common objective.
_c_	Portfolio	b.	A temporary endeavor that creates a unique product, service, or result.
_a_	Program	c.	Collection of programs or projects that achieve an organization's strategic business objectives.

3. Which is a project management process?

   a) Verification

   b) Prototyping

   ✓ c) Planning

   d) Designing

4. True or False? A project deliverable requires the approval and sign-off of project stakeholders.

   ✓ True
   __ False

5. Which project management process allows you to identify problems and take corrective action?

   ✓ a) Monitoring and Controlling

   b) Execution

   c) Planning

   d) Initiation

6. **In which project management process will you define a project's objectives and plan for the course of action to be taken?**

    a) Initiation

    b) Execution

    c) Monitoring and Controlling

    ✓ d) Planning

Activity 1-3

1. **What skills do you require to ensure that the team is not bogged down by the market expectations and the superiority of Francesca Tosca?**

    a) Culinary skills

    ✓ b) Good communication and negotiation skills

    ✓ c) Ability to motivate the team

    d) Complete project management knowledge

2. **Francesca Tosca's popularity and her celebrity status may create a rift in the team if the rest of the team finds it difficult to handle her. In such a situation, what will be your role as project manager?**

    ✓ a) Build the team as a disciplined unit that is focused on achieving the requirements of the project.

    ✓ b) Resolve conflicts that may arise in the project.

    c) Proactively communicate project information to the project team.

    d) Manage the overall schedule of the project to ensure its successful completion on time.

3. **The cookbook team involves resources who perform different functions. Which organizational structure will give you the greatest control over the entire team?**

    a) Composite

    b) Functional

    c) Matrix

    ✓ d) Projectized

4. **Francesca Tosca's TV schedules may frequently interfere with your project's schedules and affect the working hours of the other resources. What roles do you need to play to resolve this problem?**

    ✓ a) Manage the overall schedule of the project so that Francesca's TV schedules do not hamper the successful completion of the project.

    b) Proactively communicate project information to the project team and the stakeholders.

    ✓ c) Coordinate resources and motivate them to work toward the success of the project, in spite of the issues about the availability of the chef.

    d) Identify the impact of the project on the organization's strategic plans.

Lesson 1 Follow-up

Lesson 1 Lab 1

1. Which term is used to refer to work that is ongoing and produces the same outcome every time it is carried out?

    a) Program

    b) Portfolio

    c) Project

    ✓ d) Operational task

2. Which stakeholder provides the financial assistance during a project's life cycle?

    a) Customer

    b) Project manager

    ✓ c) Sponsor

    d) Project management team

3. Which project management process defines a project and authorizes its start?

    a) Planning

    b) Execution

    ✓ c) Initiation

    d) Monitoring and Controlling

4. In which organizational structure are employees grouped based on their area of expertise?

    a) Projectized

    ✓ b) Functional

    c) Matrix

    d) Composite

5. Which is a function of the PMO?

    a) Approve project deliverables at every stage of a project.

    ✓ b) Supervise and coordinate management of all projects.

    c) Provide the funds required to complete a project.

    d) Provide resources required to complete a project.

Lesson 2

Activity 2-1

1. Which are out of scope for the Italian cookbook project?

    ✓ a) A recipe for Fettucine Alfredo, Mme. Tosca's favorite Northern Italian pasta.

    b) Recipes for Southern Italian dishes that Mme. Tosca served at dinner parties she catered for visiting dignitaries.

    ✓ c) The traditional breakfast food of Southern Italy.

    ✓ d) The traditional breakfast food of Northern Italy.

2. Which is not a constraint to the cookbook project?

    a) Start and end date of the project

    ✓ b) Schedule milestones

    c) Budget allotted to the project

    d) Page limit set for the book

3. True or False? Things that limit the handling of a project are called constraints?

    ✓ True

    ___ False

4. True or False? Objectives of a project need not necessarily be measurable.

    ___ True

    ✓ False

5. Which should not be captured while examining the scope of the project?

    a) Project assumptions

    ✓ b) The ways in which the project team will accomplish its objectives

    c) The benefits that the project will have for the organization

    d) Project constraints

Activity 2-2

1. If you were the project manager for the Italian cookbook project, how will you respond to the blank spaces?

    Answers will vary, but should include the options of adding team members with the missing skills or provide training for team members.

Project Management Fundamentals: (Second Edition)

2. **Warren Scarpia is not in a position to continue in the team due to unavoidable circumstances. The management is now contemplating the right person to take his position and complete the tasks. Who do you think will be the right person to replace Warren Scarpia?**

    a) Jane Walker

    b) Carl Cavarradossi

    ✓ c) Sandra Oldenberg

    d) Andrea Ben

3. **True or False? Recruiting people with the competencies listed against the empty team member spaces in the team skills matrix will help fill the empty spaces in the matrix.**

    ✓ True

    ___ False

4. **Which team member can assist in both cooking and baking when under supervision?**

    a) Sandra Oldenberg

    ✓ b) Carl Cavarradossi

    c) Jane Walker

    d) Andrea Ben

5. **What are the uses of a team skills matrix?**

    a) Identify the availability of team members.

    ✓ b) Identify which team members have the required skillsets.

    ✓ c) Break out skills needed for each project task.

    ✓ d) Identify criteria that may be used to determine whether a team member has a particular skillset.

Activity 2-3

1. **What do you think are some of the potential risks for the cookbook project?**

    a) Behavior of the team members

    ✓ b) Availability of Mme. Tosca

    c) Paper quality of the cookbook

    ✓ d) Availability of adequate kitchen facilities for cooking and testing recipes

2. **Under which risk type will you categorize the risk of unavailability of Mme. Tosca?**

    a) Physical

    b) Environment Risk

    ✓ c) People Risk

    d) Technology

3. **Under which risk type will you categorize the risk of stakeholders disagreeing to project goals and objectives?**

    ✓ a) Organizational

    b) Law or Contract

    c) Finance

    d) People

4. **True or False? The probability of risk over an event is maximum during the initial stages of a project.**

    ___ True

    ✓ False

Lesson 2 Follow-up

Lesson 2 Lab 1

1. **Betty is clueless about the requirements of the project. What step does Betty need to take to get the requirements clarified? As it is a small project for the company's internal use, can she just assume the requirements or is there any other way she can get a better idea of the requirements?**

    Betty can discuss the requirements of the project with Rita and get a clear idea about the project's objectives.

2. **Is it necessary for the scope statement to identify what features the new system will not support? Is it important for Betty to document this? If so, what can she do to come to a conclusion about what features the new system will provide and what it will not?**

    Betty can consult John who is aware of the technical aspects of the project. The inputs will help her author the project's scope statement.

3. **Apart from the scope, what other constraining factors does Betty need to take into account? Do you think a clear understanding of project constraints is essential to complete a project successfully? Why?**

    Apart from understanding the project scope and requirements such as its technical and historical information, Betty also needs to consider the project constraints such as the project cost, quality, and the time she would take to complete the project. Without this information, the scope statement will not be complete. Additionally, these inputs will help her effectively plan the resources for the project.

4. **Once the scope statement is ready, can Betty develop the project plan? Does she need to obtain the stakeholder's approval before starting work on the plan? How important is this approval going to be?**

    It is necessary that a scope statement should get a sign-off from the project stakeholders, sponsors, and contractors. Obtaining this approval prevents untimely changes or rework in the project plan and ensures that Betty is taking the right path.

5. How will Betty know what resources she requires for this project? Is there any way she can help the management identify the skills required to complete the project work?

As soon as the scope statement is ready, Betty can, with the help of John, create a list of people required and a matrix that maps the resources to their skills. The matrix she creates may also contain the level of skills, education, and experience each resource should have. In this way, she can assist the management in identifying the required skills.

Lesson 3

Activity 3-1

1. As a project manager, you are asked to decompose the "First draft" subproject. What is the task you would be doing?

    a) Assign cost values to each deliverable.

    b) Arrange the deliverables into categories, based on risk.

    ✓ c) Breakdown the deliverables of the subproject into smaller components.

    d) Organize deliverables based on which team is responsible for their completion.

2. What WBS components will you obtain after the first level of decomposition of the "First draft" subproject?

    a) Shoot photos, obtain approval, and reshoot photos that require revisions.

    b) Create an attractive page layout and assemble the recipes.

    ✓ c) Create recipes and write anecdotes.

    d) Test recipes and edit them.

3. Which components will make up the next level of decomposition of the "Create recipes" component?

    ✓ a) Write up recipes using US metrics.

    ✓ b) Test recipes for accuracy and taste.

    ✓ c) Revise recipes.

    d) Write notes about the exotic ingredients used in the recipes.

4. Which components will make up the next level of decomposition of the "Write anecdote text" component?

    ✓ a) Collect anecdotes.

    ✓ b) Write up anecdotes.

    ✓ c) Incorporate Francesca Tosca's revisions to the anecdotes.

    d) Write up a page about Francesca Tosca and her reputation.

Activity 3-2

1. You need to add an additional Task 7 to the network diagram. Task 7 must not begin until Task 6 is complete and Task 5 is dependent on Task 7. Which would be the most appropriate location for this task in the network diagram? Sketch your answer.

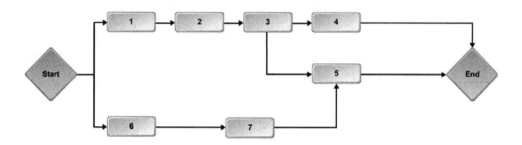

The completed network diagram should look like this.

2. You need to add an additional Task 8 to the network diagram. Task 8 does not begin until tasks 4 and 5 are complete. Which would be the most appropriate location for this task in the network diagram? Sketch your answer.

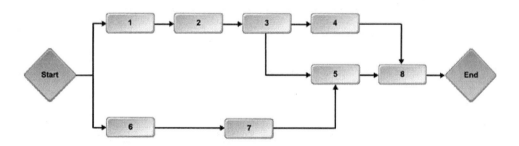

The completed network diagram should look like this.

3. According to the project schedule network diagram, which is Task 3's predecessor activity?
    a) Task 5
    b) Task 6
    ✓ c) Task 2
    d) Task 4

Project Management Fundamentals: (Second Edition)

4. What task can be done in parallel with Task 1?

   a) Task 4
   b) Task 3
   ✓ c) Task 6
   d) Task 2

Activity 3-3

1. In the given project schedule, the ES value of Task 1 is 0 and duration is 5. What will be the calculated EF value of Task 1? Sketch your answer in the diagram provided.

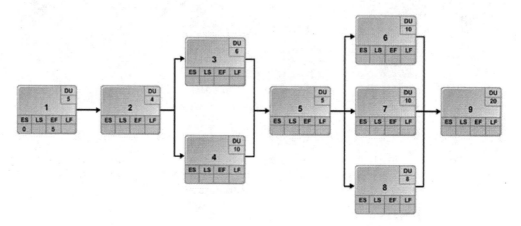

The early finish of Task 1 = Duration of Task 1. Therefore, the EF value of Task 1 is 5. The EF value is added to the diagram above.

2. What will be the early start value of Task 2?

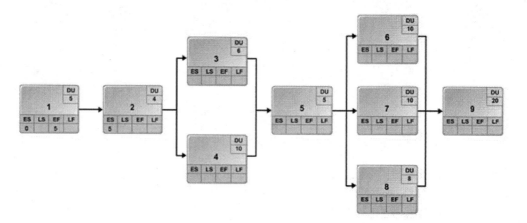

The early start of Task 2 = The early finish of Task 1. Therefore, the ES value of Task 2 is 5. The ES value is added to the diagram above.

130 Solutions

3. **Calculate the early finish value of Task 2, given the early start value is 5 and duration is 4.**

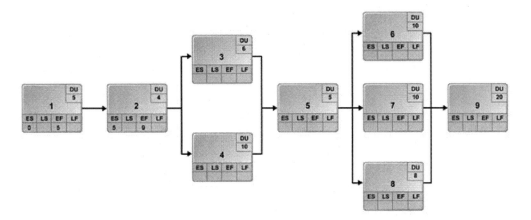

The early finish of Task 2 = The early finish of Task 1 + Duration of Task 2. Therefore, the EF value of Task 2 is 9. The EF value is added to the diagram above.

4. **Consider the early finish value of Task 2 as 9, the duration of Task 3 as 6, and the duration of Task 4 as 10. What will be the early start and early finish values of tasks 3 and 4?**

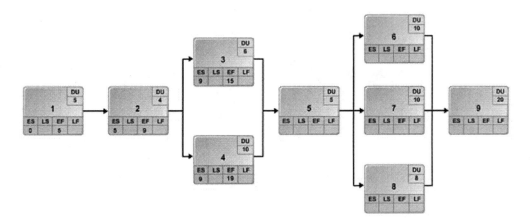

The early start of tasks 3 and 4 = The early finish of Task 2. Therefore, the early start of tasks 3 and 4 is 9. The early finish of Task 3 = The early start of Task 3 + Duration of Task 3 and the early finish of Task 4 = The early start of Task 4 + Duration of Task 4. Therefore, the early finish of tasks 3 and 4 are 15 and 19. The ES and EF values are added to the diagram above.

5. What will be the early start and early finish values for Task 5?

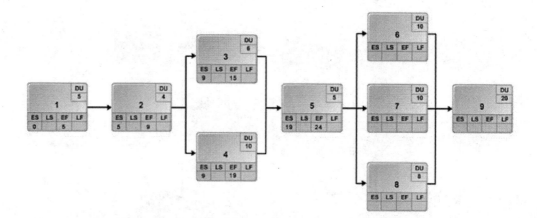

The early start of Task 5 = Maximum early finish values of tasks 3 and 4. The early finish of Task 5 = The early start of Task 5 + Duration of Task 5. Therefore, the early start and early finish values of Task 5 are 19 and 24. The ES and EF values are added to the diagram above.

6. What are the early start and early finish values of tasks 6, 7, 8, and 9?

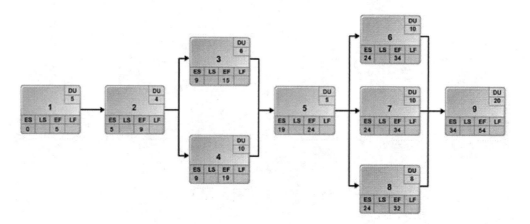

The early start and early finish values of tasks 6, 7, 8, and 9 can be calculated as before. The early start values of tasks 6, 7, 8, and 9 are 24, 24, 24, and 34. The early finish values of tasks 6, 7, 8, and 9 are 34, 34, 32, and 54. The ES and EF values are added to the diagram above.

7. **For Task 9, the early start value is 34 and early finish value is 54. What will be the calculated late finish value of Task 9?**

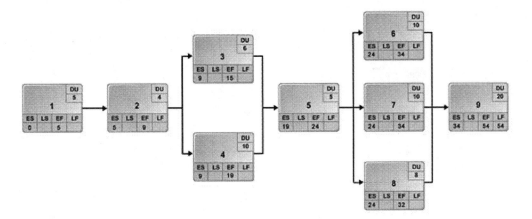

The late finish of Task 9 = The early finish of Task 9. Therefore, the LF of Task 9 is 54. The LF value is added to the diagram above.

8. **The late finish value of Task 9 is 54. What is the late start value of Task 9?**

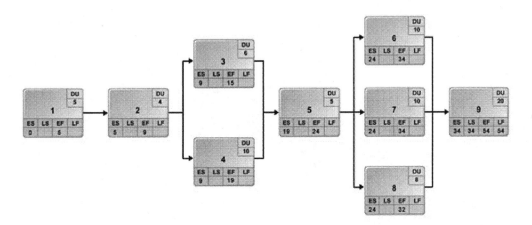

The late start value of Task 9 = The late finish value of Task 9 − Duration of Task 9. Therefore, the LS value of Task 9 is 34. The LS value is added to the diagram above.

9. What are the late finish and late start values of Task 8?

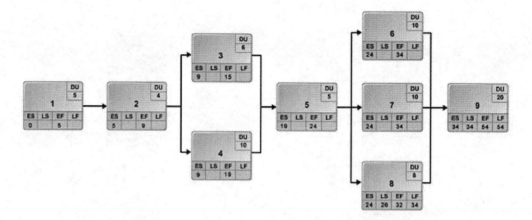

The late finish of Task 8 = The late start of Task 9 and the late start of Task 8 = The late finish of Task 8 − Duration of Task 8. The LS and LF values are added to the diagram above.

10. What are the late finish and late start values for tasks 6 and 7?

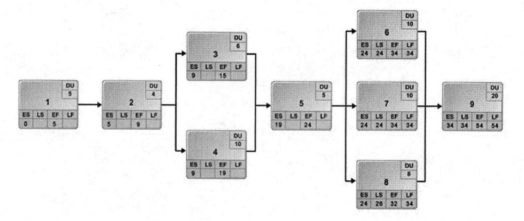

Calculating the LF and LS values is similar to the earlier steps. The late start for tasks 6 and 7 is 24. The late finish for tasks 6 and 7 is 34. The LS and LF values are added to the diagram above.

11. What are the late finish and late start values for Task 5?

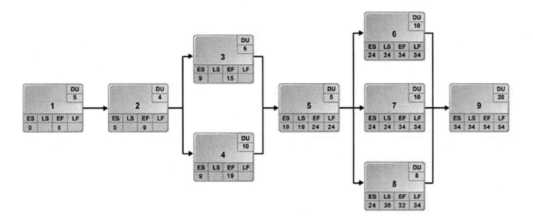

The late finish of Task 5 = Minimum late start values of tasks 6, 7, and 8. The late start of Task 5 = The late finish of Task 5 − Duration of Task 5. The LS and LF values are added to the diagram above.

12. What are the late finish and late start values for tasks 1, 2, 3, and 4?

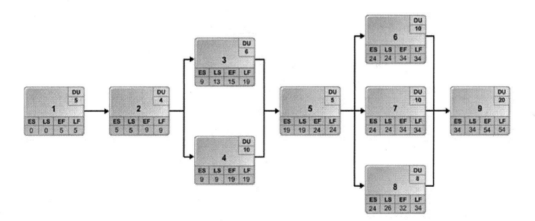

The completed schedule diagram is given above.

13. Which is the critical path for this project?

    a) 1, 2, 4, 5, 8, 9

    b) 1, 2, 3, 5, 6, 9

✓ c) 1, 2, 4, 5, 6, 9

    d) 1, 2, 3, 5, 8, 9

14. What is the duration of the critical path?

✓ a) 54

    b) 56

    c) 52

    d) 50

15. Which activities in the project do not fall on the critical path?

   a) Task 6

   b) Task 4

   ✓ c) Task 3

   ✓ d) Task 8

Activity 3-4

1. What information does the cost estimate of an activity in the project convey?

   a) The cost incurred by the activity in a similar past project.

   ✓ b) The estimated cost of resources required to perform the activity.

   c) The project's budgeted cost.

   d) The pay received by each resource per hour.

2. True or False? During the cost budgeting of the Italian cookbook project, you need to take Francesca Tosca's contract information into account.

   ✓ True

   ___ False

3. Upon cost budgeting the Italian cookbook project, what important analyses can the stakeholders perform?

   ✓ a) Assess the financial feasibility of the project.

   b) Determine market demand for the book.

   ✓ c) Determine additional funding requirements.

   d) Identify the risks to the project.

Lesson 3 Follow-up

Lesson 3 Lab 1

1. The scope statement does identify the project deliverables. But, what is the best possible way to organize the project work?

   Identifying the work components and then planning their execution is probably the best way to organize project work. Work can be broken down into sub tasks and organized into a Work Breakdown Structure (WBS). These can then be incorporated into the project schedule.

2. How would Betty know that the level of decomposition in the WBS is sufficient?

   Do you think John and Annie can help her in identifying the lowest possible amount of work?

   To check if the level of decomposition in the WBS is sufficient, Betty must check if the lowest level component in the WBS can be assigned to a resource, cost estimated, scheduled, monitored, and controlled. If the WBS component meets these criteria, she can stop decomposition. John and Annie can help since they have experience in creating WBSs.

3. **How can Betty identify the activities in the project that cannot be delayed?**

   Betty can create a project schedule network diagram and identify the critical path. Activities on the critical path cannot be delayed.

4. **What aspects does Betty need to take into account while developing cost estimates?**

   Betty needs to use the WBS and resource requirements, involve the project manager, gather relevant inputs such as resource rates, decide on the monetary units of measurements, consider risks that can impact costs, and ensure that all the estimates are assigned to the appropriate accounts.

Lesson 4

Activity 4-1

1. **What would be your primary task while analyzing a risk?**
   - a) Assign roles and responsibilities to each team member.
   - b) Develop response strategies.
   - c) Create an organization chart.
   - ✓ d) Coordinate risk identification and risk analysis activities.

2. **Which of the risks should receive the highest priority for this project?**
   - a) Temporary loss of a team member.
   - ✓ b) Stakeholders not agreeing to the objectives of the project.
   - c) Incompatibility of team members.
   - d) Currency fluctuations.

3. **What factors should you consider while analyzing risks?**
   - a) Geography of the project
   - ✓ b) Historical Information
   - ✓ c) Probability of risk
   - d) Job Description
   - ✓ e) Source of risk

4. **Associate the risk response plans with the techniques used to arrive at it.**

_a_	The lead chef is known to have a heart condition. The publishers are concerned that their investment may be lost if the lead chef cannot complete the book due to health problems. They plan to buy a "key man" policy that insures them against loss if the lead chef becomes ill or dies.	a.	Transference
_d_	The authors are concerned that readers may not be able to find authentic ingredients outside Italy. They plan to limit the ingredients to items that can be found in a typical U.S. supermarket.	b.	Mitigation
_b_	The publishers are concerned that the cookbook will be too short. They plan to add additional photos, if the first draft seems too short by a few pages; if it is too short by 20 pages, they plan to add additional white space in the margins and increase the font size. If it is too short by more than 20 pages, they plan to resubmit it to the authors and request additional recipes.	c.	Acceptance
_c_	The authors are concerned that new cooks may not know common cooking techniques like how to baste a roast or how to whip cream. They plan to assume that most of their readers are advanced-level cooks who will know how to perform these techniques.	d.	Avoidance

Activity 4-2

1. **Given the scenario, what would be a good primary communication technology for exchanging project information?**

    ✓ a) Email and phone exchange

    b) Weekly meetings

    c) Voice mail

    d) Video conferencing

2. **True or False? Keeping the stakeholders continuously informed about updates and status reports are indispensable for achieving your project objectives.**

    ✓ True

    __ False

3. **After integrating the communication management plan into the overall project plan, what would be the next logical step?**

    a) Creating a description of stakeholder communication requirements.

    b) Creating a schedule for the production of each type of communication.

    ✓ c) Distributing the plan to all the stakeholders.

    d) Determining whether there will be changes to the proposed technology before the project is over.

Activity 4-3

1. **Who will you involve in the change control planning for the cookbook project?**

    a) Francesca Tosca

    ✓ b) Key stakeholders

    c) Team members

    d) Implementation team members

2. **True or False? Only stakeholders are authorized to initiate a change request.**

    __ True

    ✓ False

3. **Who would make the decision about whether or not a change is necessary?**

    a) Stakeholders

    ✓ b) Stakeholders and the project team

    c) Core team members

    d) The project team

4. **True or False? Changes in a project do not usually affect the quality of the project.**

    __ True

    ✓ False

Lesson 4 Follow-up

Lesson 4 Lab 1

1. **What would be the communication needs of your project team?**

   Communication among the team members is vital for this project because the team members are situated in different parts of the world. Therefore, Betty can discuss the communication needs with the project's stakeholders and create a communication plan.

2. **What are the challenges involved in creating the communications plan for your team? What are the facts you would take into consideration when creating the plan?**

   As this project involves team members working from different countries, the project manager must ensure that they are able to understand each others' languages. You must also ensure that the team members have the required contact information and an appropriate system for communication.

3. **Which communication technology can be used to communicate important information effectively, while ensuring that it is not lost or misinterpreted? Why?**

   As you can easily create, store, and exchange information through email, it can be considered as an effective mode of communication for this project.

4. **You have determined that there isn't a change control process in your organization. What problems could result in this situation? How do you plan to handle it?**

   Because there are no change control processes in the organization, you must first collect the required information and create a change control system. As you are the first person to create a change control plan, you cannot consult your colleagues for guidance. Therefore, you can start with identifying the probable changes that will require a management plan and collect relevant information.

5. **What are the facts you would consider when creating the change control plan? What changes would you plan for in the given scenario?**

   You need to identify a requirement for change, determine the latitudes the team would have, converse with the stakeholders and identify the responsible parties, identify the means of approving the change requests, and then document the change control system you have identified. You realize that you may encounter unanticipated changes in the project baselines. Therefore, you decide to create a change control plan to manage it.

Lesson 5

Activity 5-1

1. **You need to decide whether to host a kick-off meeting. Which should be one of your considerations?**

   ✓ a) To generate enthusiasm about the work at hand.

   b) To educate the customer about your work processes.

   c) To know external customer's expectations.

   d) To know the budget of this project.

2. **If you decide to hold a kick-off meeting, whom should you include?**

    a) HR team

    ✓ b) Sponsors

    ✓ c) All the contributors

    d) All the employees

3. **True or False? The project manager need not necessarily define the roles and responsibilities of all the team members.**

    ___ True

    ✓ False

Activity 5-2

1. **True or False? The team can go ahead with project work after Annie Hodgson, the project sponsor, offers verbal authorization to commence work.**

    ___ True

    ✓ False

2. **When you begin project execution, what should you do?**

    a) Ensure that the funding has been approved.

    ✓ b) Comply with organizational policies and procedures.

    c) Conduct status meeting.

    d) Learn who the stakeholders are.

3. **True or False? Conducting weekly team meetings helps in ensuring that the project schedule completion dates are met.**

    ✓ True

    ___ False

4. **Your team needs to design a questionnaire, which is one of the primary tasks in the project. What should you do to help them?**

    a) Make sure they finish it on time.

    b) Make sure that the questionnaire is attractive.

    ✓ c) Monitor their general work performance and keep an eye on how well they adhere to company policies.

    d) Make sure they design it the way you would do it.

Activity 5-3

1. **What is the earned value for this work package?**

    a) $7,500

    b) $5,000

    ✓ c) $3,000

    d) $2,500

2. Calculate planned value for the "Develop Recipes" work package for the actual number of days.

   a) $2,500
   b) $500
   c) $4,500
   ✓ d) $5,000

3. What is the cost variance for the work package?

   a) $3,000
   b) $2,500
   c) $1,000
   ✓ d) $500

4. What does the cost variance indicate?

   a) The project is over budget by $500.
   ✓ b) The project is under budget by $500.
   c) The project is over budget by $2,500.
   d) The project is under budget by $2,500.

5. What formula would you use to calculate SPI?

   a) EV-PV
   ✓ b) EV/PV
   c) EV-AC
   d) EV/AC

6. Calculate the CPI for the project.

   a) 1.4
   b) 0.1
   ✓ c) 1.2
   d) 0.2

7. What does the Cost Performance Index (CPI) of 1.2 for the project indicate?

   ✓ a) The project is performing under budget.
   b) The project is performing over budget.
   c) The project is within budget.
   d) The project is behind schedule and is over budget.

8. True or False? SPI of 1.0 means the project is right on schedule.

   ✓ True
   __ False

9. **Identify a benefit of conducting the earned value analysis.**

    a) It provides a more accurate project baseline than other tracking methods.

    ✓ b) It allows you to track project performance and also acts as a means to forecast project performance.

    c) Management can understand earned value analysis better than other measures.

    d) Helps identify what the project team has accomplished so far.

10. **Your team has been working in tandem ever since the project started. But, over the past couple of weeks you have observed a dip in performance. What steps can you take to help the team perform better?**

    a) During team meetings, shower praise on members who performed well and condemn the nonperformers.

    b) Tighten the deadlines to improve productivity.

    ✓ c) Encourage team members to share their experiences with others.

    ✓ d) Appreciate good efforts during team meetings and organize events for recognizing team members who have performed well.

Activity 5-4

1. **What information does a status report convey to the stakeholders?**

    a) The exemplary performance of one of the assistant chefs.

    b) A prediction of the final cost the project will incur.

    ✓ c) A description of the project costs and schedules for the current reporting period.

    d) The conflicts between the team members and how the project manager resolved them.

2. **What is a benefit of a project forecast report to the project team and the senior management?**

    a) Pinpoints the problem areas of the project.

    ✓ b) Identifies where the project will stand if it progresses at the current rate.

    c) Identifies the team members responsible for the projected success or failure of the project.

    d) Analyzes the status of the project as against original plans.

3. **True or False? Personnel evaluations help to identify the training requirements of a project team.**

    ✓ True

    __ False

Activity 5-5

1. The IT department informs you that the project software upgrade will have a significant delay in delivery. The software includes many new enhancements that will replace the current project management information system reporting process and should be included in the training. In the risk management plan, you accounted for a delay due to the software upgrade, but this delay is much longer than originally anticipated. What action should you take?

    a) Bring information to all the team members for evaluation.

    b) Coordinate changes across knowledge areas.

    ✓ c) Identify corrective action to be taken to resolve the problem.

    ✓ d) Bring information to all the key stakeholders.

    e) Update the project plan to reflect changes.

2. Who will you involve in the change control process for the PM Training Roll-out project?

    a) People involved in the PM Training Roll-out project.

    b) All the team members.

    ✓ c) Key stakeholders.

    d) Implementation team members.

3. True or False? Change requests should be justified before analysis.

    ✓ True

    ___ False

Lesson 5 Follow-up

Lesson 5 Lab 1

1. How would you indicate the start of the project to the team members? Who are the others whom you would keep informed about the fact that the project has started?

    Betty can initiate a kick-off meeting. She can invite all the people involved in the project. She must also inform the project sponsors and Rita about the commencement of the project and tell her that the team is enthusiastic about completing the project on time as planned.

2. If a team members' availability for the project is a problem, how would you handle it?

    Requesting for additional resources for covering the team members availability can ensure that work is completed according to the schedule without any delays.

3. **In the given scenario, would it be possible to track the project progress at all? If yes, how would you be tracking the progress of the project? How will you handle variances, if any?**

   The progress of the project can be tracked by keeping in touch with the project team members regularly through phone and email. Checkpoints such as gathering monthly status reports from every member of the team about work progress can also help track the progress of the project. If there are any variances such as delays, additional resources can be assigned to cover the lag or the deliverable timelines can be extended if possible.

4. **Your project work is almost complete, but you just got a notification from the team that there may be a delay of 24 hours in shipping the content for printing. Though it is a small delay considering the amount of work that the team has put in, will it affect your project in any way? Would you discuss this with your manager?**

   Since the delay is only minor and most of the project work is complete, this delay might not significantly hamper the project delivery. It would be ideal to inform the manager about this delay, submit a reschedule request citing the reasons for the delay, and also provide information about the current status.

Lesson 6

Activity 6-1

1. **What is an element of project closeout that requires the stakeholders' acceptance?**

    a) Recipes not included in the cookbook.

    b) Minutes of all project status meetings.

    ✓ c) The final draft of the cookbook.

    d) Documentation of lessons learned from the project.

2. **What project information is important and needs to be archived for future reference?**

    a) Recipe testing activities and photo shooting activities for the illustrations.

    ✓ b) The deviations in the project schedules, reasons for the deviations, and steps taken to keep the project on track.

    c) Francesca Tosca's autograph and photographs with the project team.

    ✓ d) Variances between planned cost and actual cost, and steps taken to keep the project as much within budget as possible.

3. **True or False? You need to bring Francesca Tosca's contract agreement to a formal closure as part of the project closeout process.**

    ✓ True

    __ False

4. **What activity will you perform as part of the project closeout process?**

    a) Collect anecdotes from Francesca Tosca.

    ✓ b) Obtain a formal acceptance of the project deliverables from the stakeholders.

    c) Shoot pictures of the food cooked while recipe testing.

    d) Bring major project issues to the notice of the senior management.

Activity 6-2

1. **What information would you include in the final report of the Italian cookbook project?**

    a) A list of files and documentation generated during the project's life cycle.

    b) Documentation of the contract signed with Francesca Tosca.

    ✓ c) The outstanding coordination within the project team that ensured completion of the project on time and within budget.

    ✓ d) One of the assistant chefs met with an accident and the rest of the assistant chefs had to share the extra work among themselves.

2. **True or False? The final report is presented to the stakeholders, the project team, and the senior management.**

    ✓ True

    ___ False

3. **One of the assistant chefs was a wonderful worker. She always showed up prepared, worked hard and smart, and was willing to do more than her share of project tasks. However, she skipped or was late for at least 50 percent of the team meetings. What commentary would you include while evaluating her performance in the final report?**

    ✓ a) The assistant chef's unwillingness to participate in team meetings made things more difficult for others on the team.

    ✓ b) She made group decision making harder.

    ✓ c) She made team communication more complex, and her absence was probably a morale buster.

    d) Though she was unwilling to attend the meetings, her work compensated her behavior.

4. **What is a valid recommendation for future projects?**

    a) Hire Francesca Tosca as the chef for all future cookbook projects as she demands less compensation.

    b) Strive to complete projects before scheduled time by stretching the working time of resources.

    ✓ c) Establish a communication protocol among the project team and stakeholders.

    d) Compensate on the quality of the product if the cost to the company can be reduced.

Lesson 6 Follow-up

Lesson 6 Lab 1

1. **What elements need to be documented and archived during the closeout process?**
   - ✓ a) Documents that confirm the stakeholders' acceptance of the deliverables.
   - b) Details of phone conversations and meetings conducted with the team.
   - ✓ c) A collection of all documents prepared during the project's life cycle.
   - d) The initial calculations performed by the project manager to arrive at an estimate of the duration of project activities.

2. **Which is correct about a formal project handoff?**
   - a) It is a good idea because it covers up all the mistakes of the project team.
   - ✓ b) It can positively shape perceptions of the product by highlighting product benefits.
   - c) It should only be held if the customer pays extra for this service.
   - d) It should not be conducted if the project is terminated before completion.

3. **What information should a final report contain?**
   - ✓ a) A summary of what went right and what went wrong in the project.
   - ✓ b) A commentary on the deviations from the original plans and budget.
   - ✓ c) A record of recommendations for future projects.
   - d) A list of documents prepared throughout the project's life cycle.

4. **True or False? Documenting lessons learned and archiving project information will serve as a reference for project managers in the future.**
   - ✓ True
   - ___ False

Glossary

activity dependency
A logical relationship between two activities that indicates whether the start of an activity depends upon an event or input from another activity or an external factor.

activity sequencing
The task of identifying and documenting the relationships among the activities, and arranging the activities in a sequence based on those relationships.

activity
A unit of project work that must be performed to complete a project deliverable.

communication plan
A plan which describes what information must be communicated to whom, by whom, when, and in what manner.

cost budgeting
The process of aggregating the cost estimates of all the activities or work packages to arrive at an overall cost estimate for the project.

cost estimate
An assessment of the likely costs of resources required to complete an activity.

critical path
The path in the project schedule network diagram that has the longest duration.

decomposition
A technique for creating the WBS by subdividing project deliverables to the work package level.

duration estimation
The act of estimating the period required to complete the project activities.

final report
A report that summarizes what happened in the project.

float
The amount of time an activity can be delayed without delaying the ES of the immediate successor activity.

lag
A modification in a logical relationship that delays the start of a successor activity.

lead
A modification in a logical relationship that allows the successor activity to start before the predecessor activity ends.

performance reporting
The process of gathering and communicating information regarding the current status of a project as well as projections for progress over time.

portfolio management
Management of a portfolio to ensure that all projects in the portfolio contribute to achieving the organization's strategic goals.

portfolio
A collection of programs that are grouped together to achieve an organization's strategic business objectives.

precedence relationship
A logical relationship between two activities that indicates which activity should be performed first and which one should be performed later.

program management
Management of a program in a centralized and coordinated manner to achieve a set of strategic objectives.

program
A group of related and interrelated projects that have a common objective.

project assumptions
Statements that must be taken to be true in order for the project planning to begin.

project closeout
Process of closing out all project activities and formally ending the project or, in the case of multiphase projects, closing out a specific project phase.

project deliverable
An output from a project management activity that is measurable, unique, and verifiable.

project life cycle
The sequential phases of work done on a project, including all planning, work activities, and closure; it is marked by the beginning and the end of the project.

Project Management Office
An administrative unit that supervises and coordinates the management of all projects in an organization.

project management
The management of project activities to meet project objectives through the application of knowledge, skills, tools, and techniques to those activities.

project phases
A group of related project activities that results in the completion of a major deliverable.

project schedule network diagram
A graphical representation of the activities in a project and the logical relationships between those activities.

project stakeholder
A person who has a business interest in the outcome of a project.

project team
A group of individuals who collectively have the skills required to complete a project.

project
A temporary endeavor that creates a unique product, service, or result.

resource estimation
The means of determining the resources required to complete project activities.

risk
A risk is an uncertain event that may have a positive or a negative effect on a project.

scope creep
The additional task items that are added to a project as the project progresses and make it difficult to achieve project goals.

scope statement
An itemized definition of the agreed upon outcome of a project.

total float
The amount of time an activity can be delayed from its ES without delaying the project finish date.

WBS
(work breakdown structure) A hierarchical structure that subdivides project deliverables and project work into smaller, more manageable pieces of work.

Index

A
activities, 44
activity dependency, 44
activity sequencing, 44

C
change control plan, 75
Change Requests, 97
communication plan, 72
constraining factors, 21
cost budgeting, 62
cost estimate, 62
critical paths, 53

D
decomposition, 41
duration estimation, 51

E
earned value calculations, 86

F
float
  total float, 53

K
kick-off meetings, 80

L
lags, 46
leads, 46

O
operational tasks, 2
organizational structures, 12

P
performance reporting, 93
portfolio, 7
portfolio management, 7
precedence relationship, 45
program, 6
program management, 7
project assumptions, 21
project closeout, 103
project deliverable, 8
project execution process, 83
project life cycle, 2
project management, 6
project management life cycle, 8
Project Management Office, 13
project managers, 11
  roles, 13
project objectives, 21
project phases, 2
project schedule network diagram, 46
project stakeholders, 3
  types of, 3
project team, 27
  identifying skills, 30
projects, 2
  need for, 3

R
resource estimation, 51
risk response plan, 68
risks, 33
  identifying, 34

S
schedule development terms, 52

scope creep, 20
scope definition process, 22
scope statement, 20
  creating, 23

T

team acquisition process, 80

W

WBS, 40
  creating, 41
work breakdown structure
  See: WBS

Looking for media files?

They are now conveniently located at www.elementk.com/courseware-file-downloads

Downloading is quick and easy:

1. Visit www.elementk.com/courseware-file-downloads
2. In the search field, type in either the part number or the title
3. Of the courseware titles displayed, choose your title by clicking on the name
4. Links to the data files are located in the middle of the screen
5. Follow the instructions on the screen based upon your web browser

Note that there may be other files available for download in addition to the course files.

Approximate download times:

The amount of time it takes to download your data files will vary according to the file's size and your Internet connection speed. A broadband connection is highly recommended. The average time to download a 10 mb file on a broadband connection is less than 1 minute.